Joseph Smith's Sword

And In That Day

Miracles & Warnings

By Howard Carlos Smith

Preface

Enjoy the ride into my book. Hopefully it's a wake up call to many. It takes a glimpse into the spirit world and a ride into hell. It shares unusual experiences surrounding the Legion sword once held by the Prophet Joseph Smith. It speaks of the Prince of America with a focus upon the United States Constitution with many miracles and warnings.

Let it be known the anger of the Lord is kindled and his sword is about to fall upon the world. It is not a day of many words. It is a day where changes are awaiting even nigh at our very doors. There are no neutrals in the approaching war.

Acknowledgment

Thanks to my wife, Jolene, in helping make this book come to fruition. She has spent endless hours typing, editing and researching with a mirror of testimony into several chapters. As noted she is the co-author of this book and registered as such.

I want to give an expression of appreciation to my cousin Lamar Noble and his wife, Teri, for their support and willingness in sharing of the sacred relics. Their friendship is greatly valued.

Special thanks to our friend Lisa Dayley for her willingness to do the final editing of grammar and sentence structure.

Love sent by way of prayer to my mother for instilling within me as a lad to attend church, read good books and the value of daily prayer.

Thanks go to Blip Color for their hard work in making this book possible.

Howard Carlos Smith

Table of Contents

Voice of Thunder

Chapter 1

At sometime each of us has experienced a lightning bolt or two crackling across a darkened sky.

St. John speaks of a silence in Heaven just before the opening of the Seventh Seal. Could it possibly be the Voice of Thunder is our time period? Like a clock ticking away could a mighty earthquake with thunder and lightning be knocking at our door ready to happen? The hour and day may be upon us sooner than we think.

John's warnings from the Book of Revelation are like a large pitcher of water being poured out onto the earth all about us. None will escape. It's almost like the days of Noah when it started to rain. He was able to see wars, plagues and other events such as spirits of devils working great miracles among the kings of the earth, shortly gathering them to the battle of the great day of God. That day an angel took a censer filling it with fire at the altar casting it into the earth with voices of warnings, lightning, thunder, and an earthquake.[1]

This world is in a commotion of wars, rumors of wars, tornados, earthquakes, and other happenings. Recently a volcano erupted in Iceland spewing volcanic ash 40,000 feet into the air creating ice balls up to thirty pounds which fell down from the black cloud onto buildings, streets, farms, animals, people and blanketing the ground with thick black ash. Airports throughout Europe shut down for days, and jet pilots feared of engine failure. Powerful earthquakes shook the ground in Haiti, Peru, Mexico, Russia, China, Japan and Indonesia. Over 250,000 people were buried alive in Haiti. The USA and many other countries quickly arrived to help millions of people with food, drinking water, shelter, clothing and medical care. The earthquake destroyed the whole city of Porte-A-Prince. Recently a huge tornado over one mile wide touched down in Mississippi destroying everything in its reach as it traveled over one hundred fifty miles. A large asteroid shot across Utah lighting up the skies in several states shaking the ground. A week earlier, a larger asteroid missed hitting our earth by 73,000 miles. God is placing signs all about us, yet, the people, as a whole, ignore His warnings.

Stepping ahead to a cool summer day I'm asking my Father in Heaven to bless our family, especially Kassidy our six year old granddaughter who is visiting her Mama and Papa. My unfinished book *Keeper of the Prophet's Sword* is upon my office desk along with the Prophet's sword.

Around 9:00 a.m., after a hardy breakfast, Kassidy and I head outdoors to feed and water the animals. The sky above us is blanketed with light gray clouds, slight rain, no wind and little sunshine. She loves to feed the white homing pigeons, rabbits, laying hens and two pasture steers. Situated around the pens are tall yellow-orange sun flowers providing shade in the heat of the day for the rabbits. The garden is full of vegetables with large squash and ripe red tomatoes. But surprisingly on this day the birds that frequent our yard are nowhere to be found. The lack of tranquility makes me feel very uncomfortable. Something is very wrong.

On such a day as this, our dogs Sage and Smoky like to follow us around while we feed the animals. On this day they are missing; where are they? Thinking back to the day, I now realize that their absence was a means of warning us to exit the yard. Not known to me, an unusual event is just about ready to burst upon us.

There are no signs of lighting. It is a slightly raining day with a peaceful silence. The only exception is the lack of a breeze. Such is highly unusual for this area especially when there is cloud cover. We live in a valley where the trees point to the east.

Kassidy quickly gathers the chicken eggs, and we exit the garden area walking between the large Russian Olive and pine trees making our way to turn off the well pump. Kassidy always follows behind me, so there is no reason for me to look backward. Our backyard lawn area is outlined with many tall pine trees and a cedar fence serves as a wind break. Beyond the top of the fence is farm ground planted with sugar beets. The beets blanket the ground in dark green nearly two feet high for acres. Nearing the well pump a mind boggling event is about to burst upon us.

In the words of Robert L. Simpson: *How can any man look into the heavens and witness the order of his creations, without hearing that knock? How can any witness the wonders of this electronic and nuclear age without hearing the knock?*[2]

As I walked toward the well pump, I suddenly felt very uneasy. I stop dead in my tracks turning around to face my granddaughter. Kassidy also felt uneasy and turned around. At that moment we both look directly into heaven above witnessing a brilliant bright lightning strike almost in our face. It was about sixty feet away spanning between two pine trees slightly beyond the cedar fence. The bolt is almost thirty-five feet at its base going straight as an arrow into a whitish-gray cloud above us. Its whiteness and power is beyond any earthly description. It seemed like I was standing in the center of a tornado looking up. Slightly unnoticed was a white ring encircling us on the ground.

Almost instantly a Voice of Thunder violently shakes the earth beneath our feet, and we are hardly able to stand. I think we are dead. There is no way we could be alive with the closeness of the strike. Suddenly unexpectedly, a second lightning strike bolts out from the sky above crossing the side yard fence hitting next to our mailbox. Wow! Again thunder knocks loudly at our door shaking the ground. Realizing we are alive, I quickly grab my granddaughter into my arms making a beeline into our house. The light of the day is upon us, and it is over.

Kassidy is shaken with fear wanting her Mama so I telephone my wife who is in a business meeting. Kassidy talks with her, and Jolene comes home. Shortly thereafter, Jolene went back to her office taking Kassidy with her. About an hour later she calls to tell me that I need to come to her office and see a picture that Kassidy has drawn on a whiteboard regarding the lightning strike. Climbing into my truck I head out to the office wondering what in the world is going on. It's been such a strange day.

On this day only one other lightning strike was reported. It was near the radio station in Rupert. Standing in our yard viewing all directions, I am stunned to think that our place was singled out for a Voice of Thunder. How could this be? Kassidy and I viewed no other lightning strikes. Even to this day it's a marvel to me that we had such an overwhelmingly remarkable event.

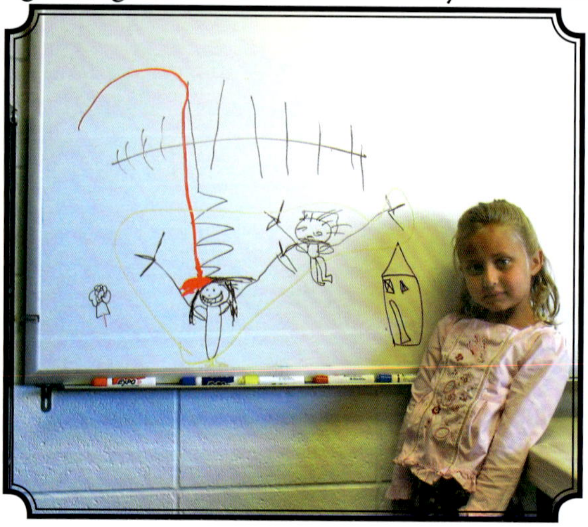

Jolene tells of Kassidy drawing a picture: "Kassidy and I went back to my office. Kassidy asked if she could draw pictures on a whiteboard in the conference room. About ten minutes later she comes out from the conference room grabbing my hand asking me to come see a picture that she has drawn. This picture is quite detailed. As I questioned Kassidy about the artwork, she told me these things. 'Papa is close to the house and well pump. Both of our arms are out because we are afraid of the lightning strike. The ground shook. The zigzag line coming to me is the ground shaking. The red line is the lightning bolt coming from behind the fence.' I asked her what the yellow was encircling her and Papa. She said, 'It was a shield that Heavenly Father and an angel placed around me and Papa so we didn't get hurt or die'. What an amazing child! To be so spiritually in tune that she would feel and see the shield and an angel. Oh the faith of a child and what we can learn from them. As we talked I explained that she and Papa were so lucky to have a guardian angel there to protect them. I was amazed to hear that it was not amazing to her.

"She's had some medical issues over the years, and I now realize that she has had previous experiences with angels comforting her. I then told her I was going to call Papa so he could see her picture. Shortly afterward Howard came to my office, and we discussed Kassidy's picture. In the *Book of Mormon,* Alma 37:6 states: *... by small and simple things are great things brought to pass; and small means in many instances doth confound the wise."*

NOTES:

1. New Testament, Revelation 8:3-5
2. Robert L. Simpson, Member of the Presiding Bishopric, 'He Knocks – We Open The Door', The Era, Dec. 1962, p. 947.

I Stand All Amazed Chapter 2

Jesus Christ "came into the world" . . . to be crucified for the world and to bear the sins of the world, to sanctify the world and to cleanse it from all unrighteousness; that through him all might be saved.[1] The atonement and resurrection of Jesus Christ is the most important event that has ever occurred in the history of mankind.

In early April, we were invited to Nauvoo Illinois. We made the trip from Idaho to Illinois, and within our car were the sacred relics of the prophet Joseph Smith. Many miracles happened along the way as well as on the return trip home. We were invited to speak at two firesides. The first one was at Winter Quarters, Nebraska, and the other at the Church of Jesus Christ of Latter-day Saint Wardhouse in Nauvoo, Illinois. Many people gathered to view the relics and to hear the story regarding them. These eleven days were truly a wonderful event. We made many new friends, and the Spirit was abundant.

I am now turning the 'proverbial pen' over to my wife who will share two of the miracles we experienced while making the journey.

"It was the second day of our journey toward Nauvoo Illinois. I was in the drivers' seat as Howard was not feeling well. As we approached the state borders of Wyoming and Nebraska Howard saw what he thought to be an extremely large statue of Jesus Christ. The arms were outstretched beaconing all to come and see the statue. We decided to do just that, and we stopped in Pine Bluffs, Wyoming.

"When we arrived to the area of the statue we found that it was a shrine to Mary the Mother of Jesus Christ. The large statue beaconing us to come was that of Mary. There were six smaller statues of Mary – three of which had the Christ Child with Mother Mary. We were absolutely amazed with the dedication of love from those who made this shrine, and I took many pictures. Out in the field among the weeds are the "Stations of the Cross" or the "Passion of Christ" made up of fourteen plaster statues. I did not know that it was called the "Stations of the Cross" until I mentioned it to our son Anthony, and he explained more about the statues. For those of you who are not knowledgeable of this history let me give you a brief synopsis. The Stations of the Cross (or Way of the Cross) is also called the Way of Sorrows (or simply, The Way) and refers to the depiction of the final hours (or Passion) of Jesus, and the devotion commemorating the Passion. The object of the

Stations is to help the faithful to make a spiritual pilgrimage of prayer, through meditating upon the chief scenes of Christ's sufferings and death. The Stations depict the following scenes: 1) Jesus is condemned to death; 2) Jesus is given his cross; 3) Jesus falls the first time; 4) Jesus meets His Mother; 5) Simon of Cyrene carries the cross; 6) Veronica wipes the face of Jesus; 7) Jesus falls the second time; 8) Jesus meets the daughters of Jerusalem; 9) Jesus falls the third time; 10) Jesus is stripped of His garments; 11) Crucifixion: Jesus is nailed to the cross; 12) Jesus dies on the cross; 13) Jesus' body is removed from the cross (Deposition or Lamentation); 14) Jesus is laid in the tomb and covered in incense. Although it is not traditionally part of the Stations, the Resurrection of Jesus is sometimes included as a fifteenth station.[2]

"I decided to look at all the statues and take more pictures. The "Stations of the Cross" are in a half circle. The surrounding area of this shrine is commercial, open fields and Interstate 80. I read the inscriptions on the statue bases and took many pictures. Howard came, looked at the statues then decided to go back to the car because he wasn't feeling well. The weather has changed from semi-cloudy and no breeze to cloudy with a slight breeze and chilly. I told him I wanted to look at all the statues again, take more pictures in detail and then we would go. The Spirit of the Lord was so strong while I was viewing these statues that I had tears streaming down my face.

"My camera is nothing special at least compared to the cameras available for sale now. It's over 10 years old but still takes great digital pictures. After I took the pictures and while walking back to our car I quickly reviewed my pictures to make sure I had taken pictures of everything. I did not look at any of the pictures in detail at that time.

"When we arrived home from our trip I downloaded two fully loaded memory cards onto my laptop. What a surprise I beheld! I quickly printed one particular picture from my black and white laser printer and showed it to Howard and then showed him the color picture on my laptop. I had taken three pictures of the Crucifixion statue approximately ten minutes apart. The sun is in the background. The picture at the front of the chapter is one of three. I have not re-touched the picture in any way. The tractor-trailer rig in the background is an added bonus. I didn't want to leave but knew that time was ticking away, and we had many hours and miles to travel to get to our destination. The words of the Sacramental Prayer used by the Church of Jesus Christ of Latter-day Saints kept running through my mind. I knew for a surety (again) that He has taken my sins upon Him. How grateful I am for Him. I testify of Christ. He is our Savior and Redeemer. Please take some time to look at the picture under the chapter heading and feel of the spirit emanating from it. It is truly a miracle. A streak of light is stretching from the Lords' left hand toward His right hand ending in a five point star. The symbolism of this is magnificent!"

Elder Bruce R. McConkie stated: *By the cross stands his mother, with her are three other faithful women – her sister, Salome, the wife of Zebedee and the mother of James and John (who were the cousins of Jesus); Mary the wife of Cleophus; and Mary Magdaline.*[3]

Jesus the Christ: *I shall carry my cross to the place of crucifixion, where I shall die in pain and agony, die as earth's Chief Martyr. He that is not willing to take his own cross and, following me, carry it to a martyr's death on Calvary, is not worthy of me and of that eternal life my Father has prepared for all the faithful.*[4]

The resurrected Lord at a gathering near the Bountiful Temple said: *Behold I have given unto you my gospel, and this is the gospel which I have given unto you – that I came into the world to do the will of my Father, because my Father sent me.And my Father sent me that I might be lifted up upon the cross; and after that I had been lifted up upon the cross, that I might draw all men unto me, that as I have been lifted up by men even so should men be lifted up by the Father, to stand before me, to be judged of their works, whether they be good or whether they be evil- And for this cause have I been lifted up; therefore according to the power of the Father I will draw all men unto me, that they may be judged according to their works.*[5]

In the words of Elder Sterling W. Sill: *Over the centuries in the minds of millions, the cross has stood as the symbol of Christianity. The Savior himself gave us the bread and wine as emblems of his sacrifice and death. Symbols not only make ideas visible, they also make them memorable. We make the marriage ordinance impressive to our minds and sacred to our memories by a particular kind of dress, flowers, and ceremony. We try to be at our best for this particular occasion and thereby set a standard that we hope will last throughout our lives. In various ways we give visual expression and impressiveness to the invisible and the intangible.*[6]

* * * * * * * * * *

Making our way back from Nauvoo we decided to visit Mt. Pisgah Historic Site. Jolene was driving at the time and made a turn off near Thayer, Union County, Iowa. It was a beautiful day later in the morning with a lot of sunshine.

Just a little history of Mt. Pisgah; on May 16, 1846 a scout selected a beautiful site that he named Mt. Pisgah in honor of a hilltop into which Moses looked upon the chosen land.

Shortly after, a wagon train of 200 Mormons stayed there. The population grew as late arrivals joined with the emigrants. Despite its beauty it was a place of sorrow. Many of the saints weakened by exposure would die over the coming months.

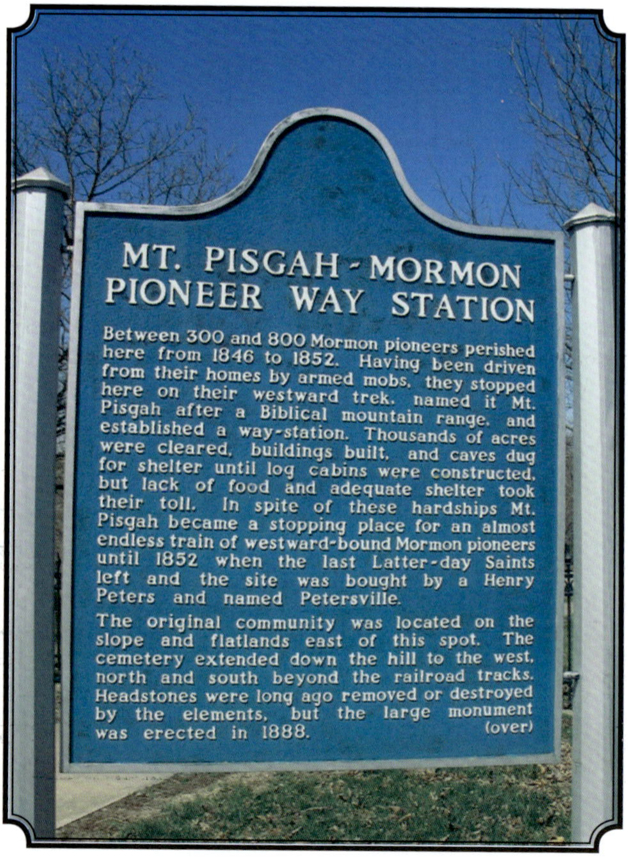

Looking collectively at Mount Pisgah, Garden Grove, Winter Quarters, Grand Encampment and other settlements over the winter of 1846-1847, many hundred perished of exposure, malnutrition and other diseases.

At Mt. Pisgah scarcely a family escaped sickness and only a few where death did not make an inroad. Samuel Smith and his family joined up with Lorenzo Snow leading a large company of saints to winter over at Mt. Pisgah. Samuel was baptized by Elder Lorenzo Snow in December 25, 1841 and they became good friends. It was a tough winter at Mt. Pisgah with many deaths including two of Samuel's children.[7]

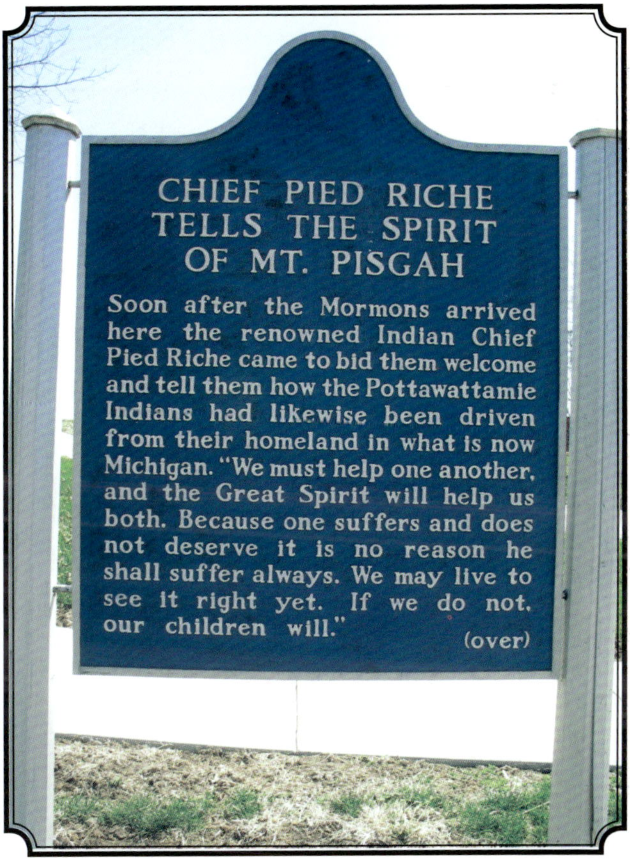

Now back to our visit at Mt. Pisgah.

As we came upon the historical site, I noticed there were at least six bald eagles sitting in the trees. We visited the memorial established for those pioneers who perished as well as the four modern day missionaries and a local member who died in an automobile accident several years ago. What beautiful country. The eagles were nesting comfortably in the trees on the opposite side of the dirt road, the sun was shining and the smell of fresh country air was invigorating.

We then decided to drive along the dirt road a short distance to view the scenery in a different location. As we drove slowly down the road, I noticed the eagles started to take flight. We drove slower so we could look at these majestic birds and noticed a pattern to their flight, they were making a wide circle around our car. It was then we realized that the eagles were keeping pace in honor of Joseph Smith and the sword within our car. I stopped so we could experience more fully this wonderful moment. I decided to get out of the car and take some pictures but before I could get the camera focused the eagles flew away.

NOTES:

1. D&C 76:41-42
2. http://en.wikipedia.org/wiki/Stations_of_the_Cross
3. The Mortal Messiah by Bruce R. McConkie, Book 4, 1981, p. 223
4. The Mortal Messiah by Bruce R. McConkie, Book 2, 1980, p. 324
5. Book of Mormon, 3 Nephi 27:13-15
6. The Glory of the Sun by Sterling W. Sill, Bookcraft, Inc., 1961, p. 258
7. http://www.webspawner.com/users/westenskow/Samuelsmithhist.html

Heavy Rain Is Falling Upon Us

Chapter 3

The day is Sunday, June 16, 1844. Gray clouds have gathered across the Mississippi River and over the city of Nauvoo. Heavy rains are falling. Two prophets – Joseph Smith and Hyrum Smith - are standing in the rain in a grove east of the Nauvoo Temple. Thousands of saints are attending this church meeting. President Smith steps forward to address his people. Suddenly the sun breaks forth and the heavens withdraw their tears.[1]

Joseph preached his last Sunday sermon at this gathering. My hand is lacking a full text of his talk.[2]

Joseph Smith may have centered his remarks upon the JST of the New Testament.

Blessed are they who read and they who hear and understand the words of this prophecy, and keep those things which are written therein, for the time of the coming of the Lord draweth nigh.[3]

But the day of the Lord will come as a thief in the night, in the which the heavens shall shake, and the earth also shall tremble, and the mountains shall melt, and pass away with a great noise, and the elements shall be filled with fervent heat; the earth also shall be filled, and the corruptible works which are therein shall be burned up.[4]

For behold, he cometh in the clouds with ten thousands of his saints in the kingdom, clothed with the glory of his Father. And every eye shall see him; and they who pierced him, and all kindred's of the earth shall wail because of him.[5]

And he shall rule them with the word of God; and they shall be in his hands as the vessels of clay in the hands of a potter; and he shall govern them by faith, with equity and justice, even as I received of my Father.[6]

Joseph Smith, the American Prophet, stands at the head of this dispensation. Someday when the veil of darkness is lifted from the eyes of the people, and they are able to see and comprehend the things of God in their true relationship, the world, will then know that June 27, 1844 marks the martyrdom of two of God's holy prophets. It was Joseph Smith who opened up the greatest of all dispensations on the earth since the world began, and Hyrum Smith, the Patriarch, his devoted and self-sacrificing brother.[7]

Shortly, the day will arrive when two other prophets will be slain. Their bodies shall lie in the streets of Jerusalem for three and one-half days. Many around the world will consider this a big event with dancing in the streets and celebrating the occasion. Many will be glad in their hearts while others will feel the rain falling upon them.[8]

Why a celebration? *These have power to shut heaven, that it rain not in the days of their prophecy; and have power over waters to turn them to blood, and to smite the earth with all plagues, as often as they will.*[9]

Pictures of Joseph and Hyrum can be viewed at the Carthage Jail Visitor Center. On a cloudy day the pictures reflect across the room through a bay window across the lawn and onto the old Carthage Jail. If you stand at the right spot in the Visitor's Center you can see Hyrum standing in the doorway of the Summer House and Joseph looking out a main floor window. It's quite

remarkable. Jolene and I were able to view this apparition while visiting on a cloudy day.

NOTES:

1. Joseph Smith Rough Stone Rolling, by Richard Lyman Bushman, 2005, p. 543.
2. Ibid, pp 543-544.
   Hyrum Smith by Pearson H. Corbett, 1963, p.373.
3. New Testament, Rev. 1:3 JST.
4. New Testament, 2 Peter 3:10 JST.
5. New Testament, Rev. 1:7 JST.
6. New Testament, Rev. 2:27 JST.
7. Elders Journal, July 1, 1906.
8. New Testament, Rev. 11:8-12.
9. New Testament, Rev. 11:6.

Common Thread David Hyrum Smith

Chapter 4

After a visit to Nauvoo my thoughts are bouncing like a basketball in different directions. For some unknown reason they are directed toward David Hyrum Smith, the youngest child of Emma and Joseph Smith. There seems to be a common thread between David and my sister Sondra even though 95 years separate their birth years. Both David and Sondra experienced a mental breakdown collectively spending many years in an institution. Each was in the prime of their lives when the disease or sickness unexpectedly came upon them. Both were married and had a family.

David Hyrum Smith, the youngest of nine children, was born to Emma and Joseph Smith on 14 November 1844 in Nauvoo, Illinois. Just five months before his birth, his father was martyred by a militia mob in Carthage Illinois.[1]

Emma Smith. Old Portrait, Artist Unknown, Ca. 1842.

David, like his father, was of a light complexion, blue eyes, tall in stature, warm temperament, quick witted, very intelligent and with a power of perception. He loved nature, the outdoors and all of God's creations. He was an artistic person noted as a poet, author and artist. He loved music writing a text for several popular church hymns such as "Let Us Pray for One Another," "Shake of the Coals." and "You May Sing of the Beauty." As an artist, he liked to paint what he knew – his mother Emma, flowers, his home as well as story illustrations such as "Lehi's Dream from the *Book of Mormon*."[2]

A list of poems was compiled in a book by David H. Smith titled *Songs of Endless Life and Other Poems*. It was published by Herald Publishing House in 1911 at Lamoni, Iowa. I would like to share one of my favorites of the sixty-four poems at my finger tips.

On Seeing A Sparrow Scratch Like A Hen

HOW now? Miss Hop-and-nip-and tuck.
Say, do you think you really are a hen?
Or are you acting Biddy? Comic struck
I watch your motions. Now you pause again
To pack what you have found there in the sand.
My! How important; at it now you go,
Flinging the dust about on every hand.
I say, Don't you think you're something though!
A thing so small to hold so much conceit
Expressed by quirking head and jerked up tail;
Ripping up gravel with your wire-like feet;
Sending it round you like a storm of hail;
"To show great things by small," as Milton says.
So now you peck again, what can it be?
Ha! Now on nimble wing you go your ways,
What you have been about I now will see.
Here is the place the gravel round you flew,
(Well on my word you are a circumstance),
While I have been here, idly watching, you
Have eaten up whole dozens of my ANTS.[3]

David shows a sense of humor and character – a witty poem – one to which a bird lover such as I can relate. A family of Savannah Sparrows like our yard and don't move on in the winter time. They like to hang around the chicken coop when the winter snows blow sharing the hen scratch with my laying hens. In good weather these sparrows earn their living scratching and ridding the yard of ants and other insects.

David fell in love with a girl by the name of Clara Charlotte Hartshorn. Both Clara and David were in their twenties and married on May 10, 1870. The two joined hands, not knowing the future or the struggles lying ahead. Soon a son arrived, Elbert A. Smith born 8 March 1871. It was a happy marriage with unity centered around their home and church.[4]

Clara remained true to David, reared Elbert and eventually died at Elbert's home in Independence.[5]

David, a baptized member to the RLDS Church (Reorganized Church of Jesus Christ of Latter-day Saints now known as The Community of Christ), was very active in missionary work. He had a deep testimony of Jesus Christ, the Prophet Joseph Smith, and the *Book of Mormon*. On the other hand my sister, Sondra Smith, (different Smith genealogy) was a baptized member of the Church of Jesus Christ of Latter-day Saints and also had a deep testimony of Jesus Christ, the Prophet Joseph Smith and a burning testimony regarding the *Book of Mormon.*

As an active member of the RLDS Church David was involved in membership and doing missionary work. As missionaries David and his older brother Alexander traveled from Nauvoo by wagon to Omaha.

Then boarding a Union Pacific Train arrived in Salt Lake City on July 15, 1869. With their Bible in hand their goal was to preach the gospel and save the Mormons. They carried a message from Emma making a visit to Brigham Young and other Church of Jesus Christ of Latter-day Saints church authorities. They preached several sermons then continued their travels into California eventually making their way toward home across Iowa, Missouri and finally to Nauvoo preaching along the way.[6]

Life moved on for David and Clara until one day he more than likely received a mosquito bite from an infected anopheles mosquito. Malaria was a common disease amongst the early Mormons in building up Nauvoo and draining the swamp lands. Once inside man, Malaria multiplies by re-entering the blood stream causing the red blood cells to rupture. The person gets chilled, suffering a high fever up to 106oF, and experiencing extreme sweating.

It is said David Hyrum Smith suffered Brain Fever and never recovered suffering a nervous breakdown, and, shortly thereafter, was committed to the Northern Illinois Hospital Asylum for the insane in January 1877. He spent the next 30 years of his life there passing on in death at age 60. Two years after his 'commitment', his mother Emma Smith died on 30 April 1879. I can only imagine the heartbreak of Emma when her youngest son was committed into the hospital, and the sadness which came upon her. Something only a mother could understand.[7]

Sondra Smith like David enjoyed the mountains, flowers and birds. At the age of thirteen she kept a diary titled "Me-Myself-and I". She said, "We enjoy going on trips together (family), taking lunches up in the mountain canyons in the good old summer time." She also had a special love for pets, especially a dog named Spot, a cat named Tabby and a yellow canary called Bee Bee given to her by Aunt Bea.

Sondra was an excellent swimmer, bowler and tennis player. As a teen every Thursday was set aside at the Deseret Gym in Salt Lake for swimming. She was also a member of the Bountiful High Bowling Club, and Saturdays she spent time on the tennis court. She loved to ice skate. In those days she would practice along the winter ice patches circling the Great Salt Lake just west of our house. Friday night roller skating at the Bountiful rink was a plus.

She was very attentive in school while growing up receiving grades averaging between the B and A range. Her favorite classes included chemistry, biology, geometry, sewing, chorus and art. She was a very smart girl making the top 10% grades in all her classes. Sondra was happy and always surrounded with friends.

She did write one poem. "He who sits on a tack is religious for he shall rise again." She stated: "My favorite programs (television) on Saturday night and Monday include "Hollywood Review – Show of Shows – Hit Parade – Mr. Penny Wood – Our Miss Brooks – Our Friend Erma – and Amos & Andy".

As a young beautiful girl, her main goal was to attend college at the University of Utah. She said, "I want to become a nurse." Little did Sondra know that a greater part of her life would be spent in mental and assisted living hospitals in the Salt Lake Valley. She spent over 40 years making hundreds of new friendships and bonding with those of similar health circumstances. Her life, just as David's, was like "on the job training" for the next life. Upon death Sondra was highly qualified as a nurse candidate for the next life.

My sister lived a full life much different than anyone can imagine. Some know her as Sandy, the girl who lived in the rest home. Others remember her as Sondra the beautiful happy girl "always with a smile on her face," who grew up in West Bountiful, Utah. She, like David, also married, starting a happy family and had a baby daughter named Julie. Sondra, her husband and daughter moved from Salt Lake City to California. She was pregnant became sick with a severe kidney infection and suffered a miscarriage. Within a few short days, she suffered a nervous breakdown.

Many of us lack compassion for those with mental sickness. We don't feel comfortable in their presence for this reason, patients hardly ever receive visits from their family members and past friends.

Nevertheless at times, angels watch over them, and their lives are for a special purpose unbeknownst to many.

Two years before Sondra passed away, God taught me a lesson regarding cats. I am not a cat lover so it was lesson time for Howard. I'm about to be taught by Mindy the cat and her keeper. At the time Sondra was living at a home operated by Valley Mental Health in Salt Lake City. Artheel Wright owned a cat named Mindy and shared an apartment with Sondra. Mindy was a large fuzzy cat with multiple colors and approaching nine years of age. One of Artheel's friends gave Mindy to her just before she died.

Mindy was very special, and, at the time of my visit, was quite sick. She liked to slip away into Sondra's small bedroom closet and sleep. Sondra with her wheel chair, and Artheel, with her attached oxygen tank, were quite the characters and enjoyed each other's company.

I showed up for a visit with pizza in hand. Sondra always referred to me as her "baby brother". This particular day Artheel was in tears as she just received medical information from the Veterinarian that Mindy would have to be euthanized. The Veterinarian gave Mindy only a few days to live.

It's now lesson time for Howard. With tears streaming down her face Artheel asks, "Howard with you being a returned missionary I have a question to ask regarding Priesthood blessings." With this statement, Sondra gets a big smile on her face. "Our Home Teachers are visiting this afternoon – would it be out of place to ask them for a blessing upon our Mindy? You know, a blessing using anointing of holy oil on Mindy."

I'm speechless for almost two minutes not knowing what to say. I'm thinking, I'm a dog lover - come on let's get real.

All of a sudden I feel the Holy Ghost come upon me. I said, "Artheel, God loves your cat Mindy, and I see nothing wrong in asking your Home Teachers for a blessing." With tears in both women's eyes they ask: "Do you really mean this?" I answered, "Yes, with all my heart." We then relaxed eating cold pizza.

Two weeks later another visit and guess what? Yes! Mindy the cat greeted me at the door rubbing against my leg. Artheel said, "Howard, we experienced a miracle from our Home Teachers. They pronounced a blessing upon Mindy, and look she's healed." Mindy the cat out lived my sister Sondra.

I'd like to share a dream. Shortly after Sondra passed away, I found myself in a large room within a spacious building. The room is empty except for a large rectangular polished wood table. Six men and one lady are sitting on tall backed chairs arranged side by side. They are apparently very busy with pen and pad in a planning meeting. As the visitor, I go unnoticed slowly walking up to face the group. The lady has a large planning book and is directing the meeting.

They're very attentive, each appearing young in age perhaps in their mid-thirties and glowing with the Spirit. Centering my eyes upon the lady I find that she is my sister Sondra. I'm in shock – what is going on and why is she here? She looks upon me smiling saying nothing but continuing on with her work. Instantly I felt hurt not being the center of her attention. After all Sondra always referred to me as her 'baby brother'. She is two years older than me with our birthdays falling three days apart.

Sondra no longer had the worn out look of spending over 40 years in rest homes. She looked like the Sondra I knew growing up. With tears flowing down my face, I was so happy to see her working away in her Heavenly duties.

I spoke up, "With all respect, each of you lack understanding to what Sondra went through during her mortal life. She is my sister – it was an extremely hard life being in a mental institution for several years and also spending many years in assisted living. Over forty years in different hospitals and assisted living. Please treat her with respect."

Spirits speak to each other by thought process almost like a pure language with little effort. It always seems very natural.

All six young men continued working on their day planner ignoring me except one sitting next to my sister. He looked up with a big smile on his face, looking into my eyes and said: "Howard you are the one lacking understanding regarding your sister. We too also spent a greater part of earth life in institutions just as your sister. She is our friend. We are planning our day to assist others in mortal life just like ourselves at one time who needed help." He then continued his work along with my sister.

NOTES:

1. "David Hyrum Smith" by Gracia Jones, 10 Dec. 2009.
2. Avery, Valeen Tippetts, From Mission to Madness: Last Son of the Mormon Prophet. University of Illinois Press, 1988, p. 52.
3. Songs of Endless Life and Other Poems, Published by Herald Publishing House, Lamoni Iowa, 1911. p. 140.
4. Joseph Smith III and the Restoration, p. 273.
5. Ibid.
6. Valeen Tippetts Avery, "The Mom's Engaging Personality", pp. 87-9, 94-8, San Francisco, CA 1965-7. Deseret News, "David Hyrum Smith" – "He was the sweet singer of Israel" by Dennis Lythgoe – staff writer July 11, 1959. Also Emma Smith Bidamon to Joseph Smith III, 5 Jan. 1877, Lynn Smith collection, Independence, Missouri.
7. Ibid.

Joseph Smith American Prophet

Chapter 5

Monday, June 17, 1844, began the final week for Joseph and Hyrum Smith in Nauvoo. The prophet sensed his doom approaching. Feeling the noose tightening, he turned the city into an armed camp. Threats from the militia mob were pouring into Nauvoo advocating extermination of the church and Joseph's death.[1]

Tuesday, June 18, he assembled the Nauvoo Legion all in military dress, with officers of high rank on decorative horses and foot soldiers standing tall. Lt. General Smith addressed the legion and thousands of people from a wood platform of a partially constructed building across from the Mansion House. The legion was 2,500 strong and ready for a fight.[2]

The body guards of the prophets are securing the area and heavily armed. Major Joseph Bates Noble, Captain Rockwell, Lt. Samuel Smith and others are like eagles glancing over the crowd in and around.

The Prophet standing in full military dress with his Nauvoo Legion sword attached to his left side addresses the legion and people. He speaks:

We are American citizens; we live upon a soil for the liberties of which our fathers periled their lives and spilt their blood upon the battlefield. Those rights so dearly purchased shall not be disgracefully trodden under foot by lawless marauders without at least a noble effort on our part to sustain our liberties.[3]

It is thought by some that our enemies would be satisfied by my destruction, but I tell you as soon as they have shed my blood, they will thirst for the blood of every man in whose heart dwells a single spark of the spirit of the fullness of the gospel. The opposition of these men is moved by the spirit of the adversary of all righteousness. It is not only to destroy me, but every man and woman who dares believe the doctrines that God hath inspired me to teach to this generation[4.]

Will you stand by me to death, and sustain at the peril of our lives, the laws of our country, and the liberties and privileges which our fathers have transmitted to us, sealed with their sacred blood? (thousands shouted aye!) It is well. If you had not done it, I would have gone out there (pointing to the west) and would have raised up a mightier people.[5]

I call upon all men from Maine to the Rocky Mountains, and from Mexico to British America, whose hearts thrill with horror to behold the rights of free men trampled under foot, to come to the deliverance of this people from the cruel hand of oppression, cruelty, anarchy and misrule to which they have long been made subject.[6]

He then asked the Nauvoo Legion: *If we loved him? If we would stand by him and sustain the laws of our country and the legion answered "Yes, yes". Then he said he was content; he would die for us. "I love you, my brethren; greater love hath no man than that he lay down his life for his friends; you have stood by me in the hour of trouble, and I am willing to sacrifice my life for your preservation.*[7]

When a Prophet speaks, listen. The words of prophecy are all about us since the beginning of time. It encircles us from all directions and is literally a knowledge of events before they transpire. These words is not speculative wherein we need to wonder or guess.[8]

The "American Prophet", Joseph Smith, unsheathing his Nauvoo Legion sword points the steel blade skyward and declares: *I call God and angels to witness that this people shall have their legal rights or my blood shall be spilt upon the ground and my body consigned to the tomb but if there is one drop of blood shed on this occasion, the sword shall never again be sheathed until Christ comes to reign on earth. May God bless you forever and ever. And we all answered, Amen.*[9]

Under the chapter heading is displayed a picture showing Lt. General Joseph Smith addressing the Nauvoo Legion. It was painted by John Hafen in 1888.[10]

At the base is a wood post just below the Prophet standing on the platform; note several somewhat evil looking characters staring off in different directions.

In an interview on May 16, 1894 a reporter for the *Republican* had recently paid a visit to the home of Mrs. Catherine Salisbury, who is a sister to Joseph and Hyrum Smith. He noted that Catherine now crowned with silver hair will be turning 88 years old in July as reported by the *Republican*.

He quoted Sister Salisbury: *I heard my brother Joseph's last sermon delivered to the great audience in Nauvoo. In that sermon, Brother Joseph said, that there was seated near the speaker stand beside him those who were conspiring to take his life, and would be responsible for his death.*

Later on Monday June 24 Mary Ellen Kimball, a sister in the Gospel, shares with us: *The last time I saw the Prophet, he was on his way to Carthage jail. Himself and his brother Hyrum were on horseback, also Brothers John Taylor and Willard Richards. They stopped outside Sister Clawson's house, at the house of Brother Rosecrans. We were on the porch. The streets of Nauvoo were narrow, and we could hear every word he said. He asked for a drink of water. They all took a drink. Some few remarks passed between them which I do not remember; after bidding goodbye, he said to Brother Rosecrans: "If I never see you again, or if I never come back, remember that I love you." This went through me like electricity. I went in the house and threw myself on the bed and wept like a child.*[11]

An article written by Arnold Irvine dated January 15, 1966 was on the front page of the Church Weekly titled *Bishop Noble – Friend of the Prophet.* Arnold Irvine states:

"Bishop Joseph Bates Noble rode toward Carthage with his close friend and leader. The Prophet rode off the road with him a short distance. The parting was a sad one. The Prophet gave the Bishop his legion sword as a token of their friendship and asked him to deliver a note to Mrs. Smith. That was the last time Bishop Noble saw the Prophet alive."[12]

Joseph and Hyrum's mother, Lucy Mack Smith, made the following comment: *My sons were thrown into jail, where they remained three days in company with Brothers Richards, Taylor and Markham. At the end of this time, the Governor disbanded most of the men, but left a guard of eight of our bitterest enemies over the jail, and sixty more of the same character about a hundred yards distance. He then came into Nauvoo with a guard of fifty or sixty men, made a short speech, and returned immediately.*

During his absence from Carthage, the guards rushed Brother Markham out of the place at the point of a bayonet. Soon after this two hundred of those discharged in the morning rushed into Carthage, well armed, and painted black, red, and yellow and in the minutes fled again leaving my sons murdered and mangled corpses.[13]

In the words of Elder B.H. Roberts an apostle to the Lord: *There is one more thought I would like to present to you respecting this Prophet, Joseph Smith. He is pre-eminently the AMERICAN PROPHET. He is not the "Prophet of Palmyra"; he is the Prophet of the Dispensation of the Fullness of Times; if localized at all he must be known as the "American Prophet".*[14]

NOTES:

1. History of the Church, Vol. VI, pp 505-14, 516-18, 528-32.
2. Clayton Diary, June 18, 1844.
3. The Fate of the Persecutors of the Prophet Joseph Smith, By N.B. Lundwall, 1952, p. 144.
4. Joseph Smith, op. cit., vol. VI, pp 473-481.
5. Keeper of the Prophet's Sword, by Howard Carlos Smith, 2009, p. 53.
6. Fate of the Persecutors of the Prophet Joseph Smith, by N.B. Lundwall, 1952, p. 153.
7. Joseph Smith – Rough Stone Rolling, by Richard Lyman Bushman, 2005, p. 544.
8. A synopsis of the speech compiled by Geo. A. Smith from verbal reports will be found in History of the Church, Period I, vol. vi, pp. 497-498.
9. JS Journal, June 18-20, 1844; JS Journal, June 18-20, 1844.
10. Daughters of the Utah Pioneers Memorial Museum, 300 North Main, Salt Lake City, Utah.
11. Juvenile Instructor, 27-490; Nauvoo the Beautiful, p. 157.
12. Special Tribute to Bishop Noble given in the Church Weekly, issue date – January 15, 1966, by Arnold Irvine of the Seventy.
13. History of Joseph Smith by Lucy Mach Smith – Mother – 1945, pp 323-324.
14. Joseph Smith the Prophet – Teacher, by Elder B.H. Roberts 1908, p. 66.

Sword In The Sky

Chapter 6

Kimberly Smith and her son Bryan Davis spent several nights as guests at our home. In early fall they left Nauvoo traveling by way of their old car with many miles heading west spreading the gospel by testimony, music and firesides. Each carrying with them the spirit of the Holy Ghost; going forth without purse or script on a mission as directed by the Lord. Upon arriving in Pocatello Idaho they shared a night of testimony at a church fireside of over 2,000 people. They then arrived at our house.

Kimberly has written a short book called *The Temple Stands,* a collection of poetry.

With Kimberly's permission I quote:

Shortly after my baptism in 1998 I began to write with more enthusiasm, and the content began to include more than just children's stories and fiction. The voices of my ancestors seemed to whisper in my heart, it was like music to my soul, and everything I wrote was like a song to me.

On a cool and misty fall morning in 2000 I visited the Homestead and family cemetery. It would prove to be one of the most special visits that I have ever had.

The geese were clamoring near the Nauvoo House, and on the river a barge moved slowly toward Keokuk.

As I watched the leaves of the trees fall softly, I grew calm and relaxed, and reflected on my great-great grandfather's days in that very spot.

Gradually I became aware that something in the atmosphere had changed. For reasons I did not know at that moment I began to cry. Such sorrow filled me and I looked toward Keokuk and then Fort Madison, and I realized I was feeling Joseph's presence nearby.[1]

Kimberly felt the presence of her great-great grandfather Joseph and may have captured a view back into time when the Prophet stood majestically one clear night viewing the stars above with his friends Wilford Woodruff and Willard Richards.

Joseph, Wilford and Willard this night saw a great streak of light in the sky in the shape of a sword with the hilt (handle) downward. The prophet told them that as sure as God sits on a throne in Heaven, so sure would there be a bloody war, and a flaming sword was a certain sign thereof.[2]

On December 25, 1832, the prophet received a revelation and prophecy on war. In Doctrine and Covenants Section 87, verses 1, 2 and 6 it states:

Verily, thus saith the Lord concerning the wars that will shortly come to pass, beginning at the rebellion of South Carolina, which will eventually terminate in the death and misery of many souls;

And the time will come that war will be poured out upon all Nations, beginning at this place.

And thus, with the sword and by bloodshed the inhabitants of the earth shall mourn; and with famine and plague, and earthquake, and the thunder of heaven, and the fierce and vivid lightning also, shall the inhabitants of the earth be made to feel the wrath and indignations, and chastening hand of an almighty God, until the consumption decreed hath made a full end of all nations.[3]

A short time after this event Joseph repeated his prophecy that the bloodshed should begin in South Carolina. He said, *I prophecy in the name of the Lord God that the commencement of bloodshed as preparatory to the coming of the Son of Man will commence in South Carolina (let it be noted that more than likely it will come through the slave trade). This voice came to me while I was praying earnestly on the subject.*[4]

Yes! We live in troubled times, however it's a great time to live and witness the events unfold as we near the advent of the Second Coming. It will be a day of great 'Global Warming'.

With permission I share with you the picture of Bryan Davis reflecting upon the spiritual journey of his 3rd great grandfather Joseph Smith in the Sacred Grove.

This picture tells it ALL and is called "REFLECTION".

NOTES:

1. The Temple Stands, a collection of poetry by Kimberly Smith, Great-great granddaughter of Joseph Smith Jr., 2002, pp. 10-11. www.ldsgenerations.com.
2. History of the Church, Chapter 5 pp. 300-301, 304; John J. Stewart, *Joseph Smith the Mormon Prophet* (Salt Lake City, Hawkes, 1966), pp 154-155. Stevenson, ed., *Autobiography of Edward Stevenson*, p. 90; See also Orson Hyde's account of seeing a glittering sword in heaven enroute to the Holy Land in Stewart, *Joseph Smith*, 154; cf, with 1 Chronicles 21:16.
3. The Latter-day Prophet – The History of Joseph Smith by George Q. Cannon, published by Juvenile Instructor Office, SLC, Utah, 1900, p. 186.
4. The Diaries and Journals of Joseph Smith, edited by Scott A. Faulring, Signature Books, SLC, Utah, p. 340.

Chapter 7

Battle At Massacre Point

It's a fall day in Idaho, the mountain leaves are turning to amber, the early morning sunshine is out, and it's time to go fishing. I load my fishing gear into the bed of my truck, pick up a few snacks at Farmer's Corner, point my vehicle towards Massacre Point and was soon there. This is my favorite spot on the Snake River; a place where the big Rainbow Trout and Small Mouth Bass linger. Lava rocks are large with water deep and sizable fish well hidden underneath the rocky edges.

Massacre Park is rich in Oregon Trail, geological and natural histories. One can access the trail from either end of the park. At times people walk down the Oregon Trail to get to the river, at other times they make their way down over many large rocks to a favorite fishing spot. It is a beautiful, serene and restful place to visit.

Over 200 species of birds have been sighted at different seasons in the park. It's not usual for me to view Canadian geese, pelicans, blue herons, and ducks of all sorts, along with deer, rabbits, coyotes, beaver, otters and other unusual animals.[1]

I park the truck off the rocky road and grab my fishing gear, making my way down off the mountain trail onto my favorite fishing rock. No one around, just me, it's a beautiful spot. A few Mallard ducks, geese and large pelicans are doing a fly by with an occasional landing onto the swirling current and scooping up a fish.

Sitting upon a lava rock with the river swirling about me, I'm in awe thinking that thousands of years ago most parts of Utah, Nevada and Idaho were under the waters of Lake Bonneville. Perhaps an earthquake or flood caused the natural dam to no longer contain the waters as the flow made its way down the Snake River. It emptied almost the entire lake in a matter of months. The Great Salt Lake of Utah is its remains. At one point an outpouring was estimated at four times the size of the Amazon River. It's likely on this sunny day I'm sitting on top of a boulder one of many ripped from the mountain sides. The water surge passed along the channels of the Snake River.[2] Wow! What an event.

Two fishing poles in hand, one is rigged for Small Mouth Bass and the other is my lazy pole. The lazy pole is the cheap pole – purchased at the local Wal-Mart store. The reel line is a 20 pound test and soon rigged with a #4 eagle hook treated with a big night crawler. I only put the barb hook up through the belly of a worm once. This way you get the full action of a wiggly worm. It's a death curl, normally called the "wiggles". As a boy, my sister, Colette, taught me the death curl while fishing on Yellowstone Lake. I believe in what you catch you eat. Nevertheless, I always follow the ruler – no bass under twelve inches. My sons have their own ways of fishing. Glenn believes in "catch and release" and is an avid Bass Fisherman. Mike is an avid fly fisherman. David is more a "catch and eat" type fisherman. Anthony doesn't fish.

With the first cast I hook into a ten pound Rainbow Trout. Wow! What a fight. It finally lands into my fishing net and then onto the stringer. I can hardly believe what had just landed into my net. This is surely my lucky day.

Sitting back on the rock I recast, letting a worm make its way deep into a hole just under my casting rock. Soon there was a little tug. A fish was on the line, however, looking around, my priorities soon changed. I'm fighting for my supper, and my only weapon is my fishing pole. A large red mink is taking off with my prize Rainbow Trout. The battle is on - fishing pole against mink. Oh! My other pole is now halfway into the river. The confrontation continues with one pole lost into the swirling water, and the other pole used as a weapon.

My fighting pole was almost like using a sword. I would hit the mink, and it would stop, hiss, show its teeth and strike again. I would hit the red mink again and again with my Wal-Mart pole. Same thing – it was a tug of war. This went on and on for almost an hour.

Nevertheless, I won the battle! Sadly however my lazy pole is extremely damaged - just dangling in parts. I felt like a hero, yet only to myself. This was truly my lucky day. Stringer in hand with a ten pound Rainbow Trout dangling on the end, carrying my gear I make my way back up a trail pointing myself towards my truck.

With a prize fish in the ice box, and, heading home my thoughts went back to a summer day in 1957. A day when my Uncle Delbert Noble sat me down under a tree next to an old adobe house once belonging to his grandfather, pioneer Joseph Bates Noble. This house was built in 1857 by Joseph Bates Noble and was located just off a dirt road named Onion Street in West Bountiful, Utah. It stood for nearly one hundred years.

On this day my Uncle Del told me a story about Joseph Smith's Nauvoo Legion Sword, the Prophet's pistol, an oak casket stick and showed me his grandfather's Ball and Cap Musket rifle. The other relics were hidden away in an old adobe house just a few feet away. My uncle Del, at the time, wanted to share with me the sword. Nevertheless, the day was late, and, at age 16, my interest was in my 1949 Ford coupe and girls. My uncle sensed this and did not pursue the subject further.

Joseph Bates Nobles' adobe house was located just across the street from my house. I could see it from my bedroom window. I could throw a rock and hit its front door. The front yard had huge trees for shade. A dirt road and small creek separated it from our side yard. On the back side of this house was the 30-acre Noble farm. We sometimes referred to it as the Indian Farm. Today the farm ground is all houses and underneath them are the memories of my youth. I worked this farm from age seven through my senior year at Bountiful High School.

Smith Family House – West Bountiful Utah

As a boy, I remember going to visit Uncle Del's parents, Wally and Lenora Smith Noble. They lived in Joseph Bates Noble's adobe house. Wally showed me a wooden box full of Indian arrow heads and other relics. They collected items over the years as they worked the farm. Wow, I was fascinated as a young boy. My great-uncle Wally told me a story about many Indians that once camped out on the farm hundreds of years ago. He said a great battle was fought upon this ground. He also mentioned that the northern end of the farm was an ancient Indian burial ground.

Uncle Del always used a shallow plow behind a team of horses whenever we worked the northern end of that farm. He also counseled us as farm hands to be careful in our planting. Nevertheless, one spring day I found a petrified human bone. I didn't keep it but instead buried it deeper into the ground. Another time I remember finding an ancient granite rock used for grinding grain. It was flat on one side with a worn thumb mark.

From 1956-1958, after Uncle Wally's passing, the old adobe house was used to store winter onions. My cousin Lamar and I used one bedroom as a work-out room. It was a small room with a stairway leading up to a locked door. No one was allowed into this room. Unbeknownst to me the sword was hidden away within this room. Lamar, being like an older brother to me, taught me the art of lifting weights. You know – it makes the biceps look good. I always felt a special spirit in the weight room.

Time marches on, and the Noble farm is now a subdivision with many beautiful houses. The wooden box of Indian arrow heads and other rock relics no longer exists and no one knows of their whereabouts.

NOTES:

1. http://www.seidaho.org/massacrerock.html.
2. Ibid.

Behold Joseph Smiths' Sword

Chapter 8

A week later my thoughts are still lingering back to the Battle at Massacre Point. We have already made several fish fry's from the large rainbow trout; twice friends have come over to join in on a tasty meal.

Well, today started out wrong! I had an extreme toothache from the top of my forehead across my face through the lower jaw and onto my lower neck. I desperately needed a dentist, so early in the morning I point my car toward Riverton, Utah. There is no hurry because I'm allowing myself six hours before my appointment with Dr. Noh, my favorite dentist.

Approaching all the wonderful traffic in Bountiful, I think its time to visit my cousin. Lamar and I are like brothers, yet it has been ten years since our last visit. Where had the time gone? West Bountiful looks nearly the same with many new houses, however, the farms are far gone. But my dad's old brick house built in 1897 is still standing. The north side of the house faces Lamar and Teri's house that is directly across the street.

I turn off Onion Street and into the Noble driveway. I am greeted by Lamar and shortly afterward we are sitting on a sofa having a cold drink. The drink doesn't set well with my toothache. Teri is out shopping, so it's just the two of us. Mounted on the wall directly above my head is the old Cap and Ball musket rifle belonging to Lamar's great-grandfather Joseph Bates Noble.

Our conversation is now centered upon this old rifle and its family history. Soon sorting through a box of old pictures Lamar shares a story with me about pioneer Joseph Bates Noble:

My great grandfather, Joseph Bates Noble, was an early convert to the Mormon Church; he was a body guard to Joseph Smith. He was also a Captain of fifty men and a Bishop. In 1841 he performed the first plural marriage in the Church marrying Joseph Smith to Bates' sister-in-law Louisa Beman.

Joseph Bates Noble was riding with Joseph Smith to Carthage Jail when Joseph took him aside and gave him his Legion Sword and told him to go back to Nauvoo. After Joseph Smith was killed, Joseph Bates Noble and some other men sneaked his body (which was in an oak box) back to Nauvoo. All the men were given a stick from the lid of the oak casket.

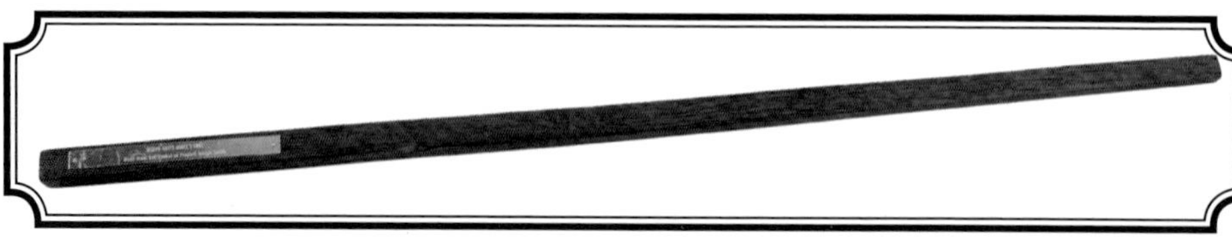

My great grandfather brought the sword, a ball and cap rifle, and the oak stick across the plains to his adobe home in West Bountiful Utah. Before his death he gave these items to my grandfather Wally. Wally lived in the adobe house until his death in 1956. He gave these items to my father who in turn gave them to me before his death in 1994. I have tried to keep them safe and maintain them in good condition.[1]

At this point and time I would like to share a short resume regarding Joseph Bates Noble. It will add clarity to his life.

At the age of 22, in 1832, he was baptized by Brigham Young.

He stayed nine days at the prophet's house. He pitched hay seven days with Joseph and Hyrum Smith. The Prophet shared many stories with Bates.

- He answered a call to serve in Zion's Camp.
- He was a Bishop of a Kirtland Ward.
- He was ordained a member of the First Quorum of Seventy.
- He attended the School of the Prophets.

- He learned several languages including Hebrew.
- He witnessed heavenly manifestations in the Kirtland Temple.
- He served as a body guard to Joseph Smith.
- He also acted as a messenger for the prophet.
- He had several visits with the prophet at Liberty Jail.
- He was a missionary in southern Ohio.
- He was healed by the prophet's hand.
- He served as Bishop of the Nauvoo 5th Ward, where President Smith and his family attended church.
- In 1841 he performed the first plural marriage for the church.
- He held the rank of Major in the Nauvoo Legion.
- He was Keeper of the Prophet's Nauvoo Legion Sword.
- He was a key officer in rescuing the bodies from Carthage.
- He was keeper of an oak casket (coffin) stick.
- He led a company of 171 Saints into the Salt Lake Valley early October 1847.
- He built the first adobe house in West Bountiful, Utah.

- He married Sylvia Loretta Mecham in January 1857. Loretta shared in building the new adobe house. They had a large family.
- Later on he served on the High Council, as a Stake Patriarch, as a Bishop of the West Bountiful First Ward.
- Joseph Bates served several missions including one to England.
- See Appendix B for wives and children of Joseph Bates Noble.

This list could go on and on. Nevertheless, it gives one a feeling as to the sort of man he was during his mortal span of ninety years. Joseph Bates Noble never once turned his back to God or his friend Joseph Smith the latter day Mormon prophet.

During our short visit Lamar, and I refreshed our drinks with a cold soda pop. It was like a nerve shot into my toothache. We moved from the living room to the kitchen table. Bogey his dog settled at the base of the table, and we continued our conversation. I asked, "What happened to the old Nauvoo Legion Sword belonging to Joseph Smith? Is it still in the family?" Lamar smiled and said, "Would you like to see the sword?" A definite "YES" came from me. The sword still in its scabbard is soon displayed onto the kitchen table. This relic has

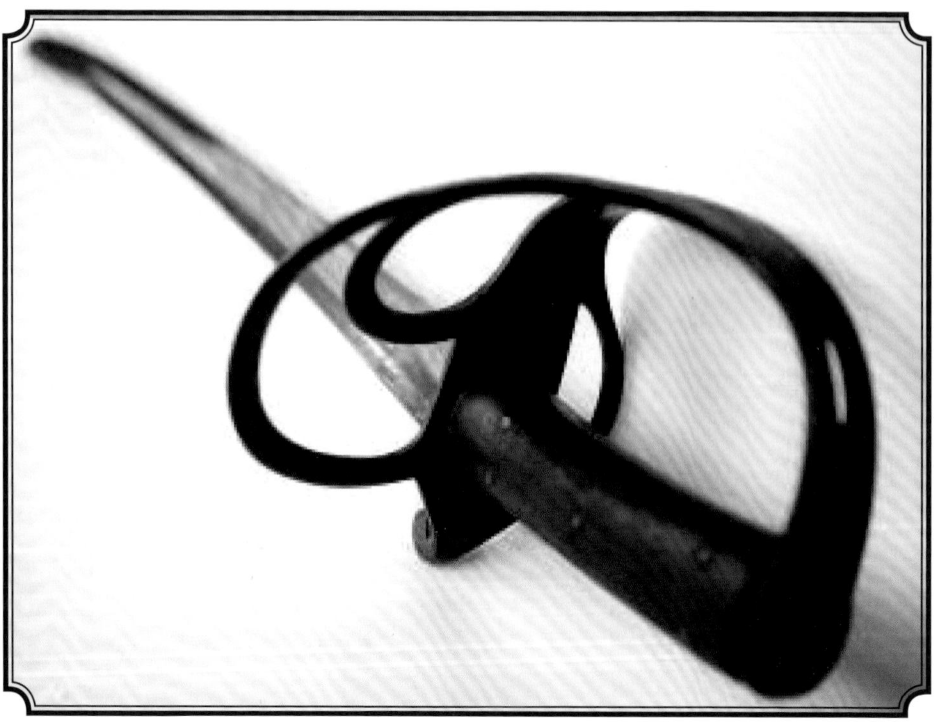

been hid away for 165 years, not on display, and few men have unsheathed the prophet's sword. I could hardly believe my eyes. What an opportunity. What an honor. Why me?

Standing near the kitchen table I unsheathed the Prophet's sword placing my right hand around the hilt handle. I felt a spirit like I've never felt before, almost like holding hands with the Prophet Joseph himself.

Thanking Lamar, I'm out the door into my Corolla pointing my way amongst the traffic toward the dentist office. Little did I realize this event would be a great changing point in my life.

NOTES:

1. Lamar Noble, great grandson to pioneer Joseph Bates Noble shares with me in the Fall of 2007.
2. Journal of Joseph Bates Noble – Autobiography Typescript, BYU-S; Overview given by Lamar Noble, great grandson of Joseph Bates Noble; West Bountiful 1848-1985 – A Pictorial History by LaRue Hergoe and Edith Deppe.

Let The Bell Ring On Independence Hall

Chapter 9

You should have heard the old bell in the belfry at Philadelphia ring out its joy when it was announced that the Declaration was signed. As fast as the messenger could ride from Philadelphia to New York, as fast as the news could be sent to Massachusetts, Virginia and the Carolinas, one after the other, the bells in all the church – steeples took up the peal of the big bell in Philadelphia and rang out the Anthem of Freedom all over the land.[1]

The Declaration was signed on the 4th of July 1776. As quick as the winking of an eye 235 years later, the bells no longer ring. Many across the land are saying, 'Remember Rome?' And others are saying 'Give a listening ear to the Father of our Nation, President George Washington in 1787.

Remember Rome? Its decline started in the hour when the cross currents of national life began to ebb and flow with a rapidity wholly baffling to the ingenuity of human leadership. Because of unholy ambitions, it was a time that people began to lose confidence in their system of government. A crisis was precipitated by the populous demanding A CHANGE. This is a typical evolution of events in a nation which is sick at heart. A nation that will not admit its growing lethargy is the result of poison issuing from within its own people. Does this ring a bell or sound familiar with our last presidential election?

Beware America. Wake Up. There is a plan to bring about a 'New World Order' consisting of a secret code noted as a one world government. It is a conspiracy between the elite progressives of this country and other countries around the world. Their alliance committees believe the prize is almost within their grasp, and they are about to make a mad dash to the finish line. If we as Americans allow this to happen, our United States Constitutions' Bill of Rights will be gone and our firearms will be confiscated just as it happened in United Europe.

The war in heaven is raging on the earth today. The issues are the same: shall men be compelled to do what others claim is for their best welfare or will they hold to the council of the prophets and preserve their freedom.[2] *Today Satan argues that men given their freedom do not choose wisely; therefore a so-called brilliant, benevolent few must establish the welfare government and force us unto a greater socialistic society.*[3]

Give a listening ear to the Father of our Nation – President George Washington, 1787:

The Constitution will always be in the people. It is entrusted for certain defined purposed, and for a certain limited period, to representation of their own choosing; and whenever it is executed contrary to their interest, or not agreeable to their wishes, their servants can, and undoubtedly will, be recalled.[4]

In 1954 a U.S. Senator, William Jenner, gave a wake up call for this day:

Outwardly we have a constitutional government. We have operating within our government and political system another body representing another form of government: a bureaucratic elite which believes our Constitution is out moded . . . all the strange developments in foreign policy agreements may be traced to this group who are going to make us over to suit their pleasure.[5]

Satan, like most dictators, perpetrated an invasion upon our rights and, even at this time, he perpetrates an invasion upon our liberty and freedoms. Progressiveness is socialism and eventually leads to the loss of freedom. It can happen quickly. Be aware of our leaders, socialized medical and medicine, government takeover of banks, car industries and our schools. Many schools today take on a progressive style and teaching methods. Just who are we fighting? *And the great dragon was cast out, that old serpent, call the Devil, and Satan, which deceived the whole world; he was cast out into the earth, and his angels were cast out with him.*[6]

He lives as a fallen angel, yet he too was created in the image of God. He will not support you in these last days, but he will speedily drag you down to hell; his world is *in the earth* and *under the earth.* Satan's mission is to take possession of this earth. It is also to deceive its inhabitants who have been sent by the Father to test their integrity. He is a master artist, and Joseph Smith states, *"... has been and still is much underrated."*[7]

It is worthy to note that all spirits, good and evil are eternal and cannot be destroyed. Lucifer was one of us, a Son of the Morning, one with authority. He was one with great power, a speaker, and an orator wielding great influence in and among all the people. We knew him. We just can't remember him. He had free agency just like us. In the great rebellion, one involving billions of spirits, he sought to destroy the agency of both man and woman. A great war took place in heaven. We were a part of that war. About one third of our brothers and sisters were cast out with him each being denied the privilege of a mortal birth.

As we near the second coming of Jesus Christ, this war will intensify more and more. Lucifer as a fallen being and his hosts became spirits of relative darkness. They lack the light of Christ in their eyes. The elements composed in their spirits enable them to appear at times to mortals as "angels of light," and "there is more or less a darkness about them".[8]

Our history of America is buried in the labyrinth of a forgotten past when the bells rang, nevertheless, how many people are aware that human life had its beginning on this continent? After many centuries of academic interest, the Lord revealed that the Garden of Eden was not in Mesopotamia as many had supposed. The Garden of Eden was here upon the North American land[9] and Adam walked and talked and taught his people here upon our land.[10]

Yes, it was here that Adam lived. Yes, it was here that the City of Enoch was built, and it was here where Methuselah lived nine hundred and sixty-nine years. It was here where his grandson Noah built the historic Ark.[11]

It was here, after the floods and deluge, that a choice group of Noah's descendants were led back to America to repopulate it. These people were called the "People of Jared". They crossed the seas in eight boats and brought with them all kinds of animals.[12]

They built a marvelous civilization upon the Americas, and it was a country greater than any contemporary kingdom.[13] The people were numbered in the millions and they existed on the American continent from approximately 2300 – 600 B.C. It's sad to say the Jaredites soon annihilated themselves through civil war.

About that same time (600 B.C.) the Lord directed another people, the people of Lehi to leave Jerusalem, cross Arabia and build a ship. They as a family successfully negotiated the trans-oceanic voyage to America.[14]

The family separated into two separate nations and from 600 B.C. – 400 A.D. they grew until their cities covered the whole face of this land. The people were numbered almost as it were the sand of the sea.[15] The *Book of Mormon* contains a history of this people.

Around 400 A.D. the two great nations met head on in a gigantic military conflict lasting sixty years resulting in the annihilation of the Nephite Nation. The victors of this war were the Lamanite Nation. Their descendants are the modern American Indians (also known as Native Americans). If you are a history enthusiast, I recommend that you jump into the *Book of Mormon* and absorb this rich history. It is a history of these people written by the prophets and leaders. It is a message for our day.

So this, the American continent has been inhabited almost continuously since man first became a resident upon this earth.

AND in that day... our day,

"Shall be heard of wars and rumors of wars, and the whole earth shall be in commotion, and men's hearts shall fail them, and they shall say that Christ delayeth his coming until the end of the earth."[16]

And thus, with the sword and by bloodshed the inhabitants of this earth shall mourn; and with famine, and plague, and earthquake, and the thunder of heaven, and the fierce and vivid lightning also, shall the inhabitants of the earth be made to feel the wrath, and indignation, and chastening hand of an Almighty God, until the consumption decreed hath made a full end of all nations.[17]

Elder John A. Widtsoe commented: *The troubles of the world may largely be laid at the doors of those who are neither hot nor cold; who always follow the line of least resistance. Who's timid hearts flutter at taking sides for truth. As in the Great Council in the heavens, so in the Church of Christ on earth, there can be NO neutrality.*[18]

President Wilford Woodruff adds his testimony: *I warn future historians to give credence to my history; for my testimony is true, and the truth of its record will be manifest in the world to come. The American nation will be broken in pieces like a potter's vessel, and will be cast down to hell if it does not repent – and this, because of murders, whoredoms, wickedness, and all manner of abominations, for the Lord has spoken it.*[19]

We live in a day where one cannot be caught in the middle of the road. You follow Christ or you follow Satan. You cannot walk two paths at the same time. You cannot serve two masters. Lucifer is the author of all lies. His mission is to destroy the souls of all men that they might be like him. He has within his hands legions of 'angels' willing to assist him in carrying out the schemes of destruction. He wants dominion over all the earth, and those of us whom dwell here. He will stop at nothing to achieve his goals and objectives. He will have you murdered, killed or thrown into prison without any consequence as to his acts upon you.

A revelation was received on April 6, 1833 from the Lord to the 'American Prophet' Joseph Smith: *I, the Lord God, make you free, therefore ye are free indeed; and the law also maketh you free. Nevertheless, when the wicked rule the people mourn. Wherefore, honest men and wise men should be sought for diligently, and good men and wise men ye should observe to uphold; otherwise whatsoever is less than these cometh of evil.*[20]

Elder Ezra Taft Benson of the Council of the Twelve Apostles addressed the Sunday Morning Session of General Conference on April 8, 1962. I quote a portion of his talk reflecting into our time.

Now God will not permit his base of operation – America – to be destroyed. He has promised protection to this land if we will but serve the God of the land. He has also promised protection to the righteous even, if necessary, to send fire from heaven to destroy their enemies. (Ether 2:12, 1 Nephi 22:17)

It was his latter-day purpose to bring forth his gospel in America, not in any other place. It was in America where the Book of Mormon plates were deposited. This was no accident. It was his design. It was in this same America were they were brought to light by angelic ministry. It was "... [here] where he organized his modern church, where he, himself made a modern personal appearance. (Editorial, Church News)

Yes, the Lord planned it all. Why? So "America" could serve as a beacon of liberty and in preparation for the opening of a new gospel dispensation – the last and greatest of all dispensations in preparation for the Second Coming of the Lord Jesus Christ.[21]

NOTES:

1. The History of Our Country, by Abby Sage Richardson, Boston; Houghton, Osgood and Company, Riverside Press, Cambridge, 1880, p. 222.
2. God-Family-Country, Ezra Taft Benson, Deseret Book Company, SLC, UT, 1974, p. 384
3. Ibid
4. The Writings of George Washington, by John C. Fitzpatrick, GPO, 1931-44. Vol. 29:311.
5. February 23, 1954, U.S. Senator William Jenner – Shadows of Power by James Perloff, (Boston: Western Islands © 1988), p.4.
6. New Testament, Rev. 12:79 and Book of Mormon, 2 Nephi 2:17.
7. History of the Church, Vol. IV, p 605.
8. History of the Church, Vol. III, p 392; Vol IV, pg 582; Also Pratt, op cite, pp 114-115.
9. Cowley, Matthias F., Wilford Woodruff, p. 481
10. D&C 116, also Discourses of Brigham Young, 1966 Edition, by John A. Widtsoe p.102.
11. Smith, J.F., The Progress of Man, p. 249
12. Book of Mormon, Ether 1:41-42
13. Book of Mormon, Ether 1:43

14. Book of Mormon, 1 Nephi 18:22-23

15. Book of Mormon- The Book of Mormon, Chap. 1:7, p. 469.

16. D&C 45:26

17. D&C 87:6

18. Conference Report, April 1941, pp 16-17.

19. Wilford Woodruff, by Matthias F. Cowley, p 500

20. D&C 98:8-10

21. The Improvement Era, June 1962 – Conference Talks – Sunday Morning Session – April 8, 1962. The Lord's Base of Operations by Elder Ezra Taft Benson of the Council of the Twelve Apostles; pp. 456-457.

Warning For Constitutional Fortitude

Chapter 10

One of my favorite U.S. History books sat for many years upon a shelf at the Sherburn Merrill Smith Memorial Public Library in Wendell, Idaho. It now honors a space in my home library. It is titled *The History of Our Country – From its Discovery by Columbus to the Celebration of the Centennial Anniversary of its Declaration of Independence;* printed by the Riverside Press, Cambridge, 1880. Truth flows from its pages like the mighty Snake River winding its way across the state of Idaho. It is a book needed as a text for our educational system covering this nations' history and as a study guide for all U.S. History classes. I must be dreaming. The thick 635 pages may be a hard read for some congressional representatives, senators and a progressive president.

Picture a teacher addressing her students, "If you were reared in the United States you will have no doubt heard of this George Washington. He was known as the "Father of this Country," and became one of our greatest heroes."[1]

Suppose a modern teacher using an old movie projector loaded with a reel of U.S. History film, such as this book, fast tracks it backward into a different time frame, stopping at the year of 1787 then slowly working its way forward. Looking upon the projection we view a convention being held in Philadelphia Pennsylvania. The signers of the United States Constitution are now in full view. A count is taken with George Washington being voted in as President of the Constitutional Convention.

Shortly thousands are gathering into New York City to celebrate the adoption of this new constitution. It is a grand procession such as never before seen in America. It is lead by a person dressed to look like Columbus, the European discoverer of our country. He is encircled by pioneers bearing axes to denote the early settlers building cabins and clearing lands. After them came the farmers with plows, scythes and reapers. Following in the procession is a baker displaying a gigantic loaf of bread ten feet high and inscribed with the names of the colonies. Several coopers binding staves of an immense barrel encircled with a strong iron hoop called "The New Constitution" as well as butchers roasting a 1,000 pound whole ox. The grand procession continues with cabinet makers displaying a "Federal Chair of State" gorgeous enough for an eastern emperor; tailors, masons, carpenters, all carried some emblem of their trade. [2]

The people along the way stood breathless looking upon the huge ox rotating mechanically upon a gear spindle above a bed of hot amber coals. The aroma of the roasted ox filled the surroundings with a pleasant smell.[3]

Following their ranks were thirteen boys, each thirteen years old, dressed in white with ribbons and garlands of green representing the thirteen colonies. Next was the ship of state, drawn on a cart by ten milk white horses. It was manned by thirty sailors, who went aloft in the rigging, furled and unfurled sails and going through all the motions in bringing a ship safely into a port experiencing fair and foul weather.[4]

The gallant vessel was presented with a flag being received with the cheers from the crowd and sailors. People by the thousands were shouting and hurrahing until they were hoarse. Finally the procession of people sat down to a banquet in a fine pavilion decorated with thirteen flags boasting thirteen stars.[5]

The projector reel stops momentarily. I can remember, as a school boy, looking forward to the birthdays of George Washington and Abraham Lincoln. It was a big event in my elementary school. Our teacher spent several days teaching us about freedom, the U.S. Constitution, a cherry tree and 'Honest Abe'.

I can still remember in vision Honest Abe under a candle light reading his Holy Bible. The small log house, tiny bedroom, a hot rock under the bed covers, the cold of night and only a twinkle of light. Yet, he took time out each night to read the scriptures. He spent many nights on his knees pouring out his spirit to the God of this earth.

President Abraham Lincoln made this comment regarding our schools:

Let the Constitution be taught in our schools, in seminaries and in colleges; let it be written in primers, spelling books, and almanacs; let it be preached from the pulpit, proclaimed in legislative halls, and enforced in the courts of justice, and in short let it become the political religion of the nation.[6]

Abraham Lincoln by Lynne Millman-Weidinger
www.millmanstudios.com

President Washington shares a vision and warning for our day: *And there is one thing I much fear, and that is, that the American people do not properly appreciate the boon of freedom... Party split is becoming stronger, and unless it is checked, will, at no distant day, undermine and tumble into ruin the noble spirit of the Republic.*[7]

You have doubtless heard the story of George Washington going into the thicket to pray. Well, it is not only true, but he often prayed in secret for aid and comfort from God.[8]

President Washington's closing remarks were: *Let her (America) remember that in union she has strength, in disunion is her destruction.*[9]

The Prayer at Valley Forge

Painting by Arnold Friberg, RSA

President Ezra Taft Benson spoke at a Brigham Young University Devotional held 16 September 1986, in this speech he said:

Shortly after President Spencer W. Kimball became President of the Church, he assigned one to go into the vault of the St. George Temple and check the early records.

As I did so, I realized the fulfillment of a dream I had ever since learning of the visit of the Founding Fathers to the St. George Temple.

I saw with my own eyes the record of the work which was done for the Founding Father of this great nation, beginning with George Washington.

Think of it, the founding of this great nation, appeared within those sacred walls and had their vicarious work done for them.

Their noble spirits came there with divine permission – evident that this work of salvation goes forward on both side of the veil.[10]

I have faith that the Constitution will be saved as prophesied by Joseph Smith.

I reverence the Constitution of the United States as a sacred document.

We, the blessed beneficiaries, face difficult days in this beloved land, '*a land which is choice above all other lands*'. (Ether 2:10) It may also cost us blood before we are through.

It is my conviction, however, that when the Lord comes, the stars and stripes will be floating on the breeze over this people.

God give us the faith and the courage exhibited by those patriots who pledged their lives, their fortunes, and their sacred honor that we might be free.[11]

NOTES:

1. The History of Our Country, by Abby Sage Richardson, Boston; Houghton, Osgood and Company, Riverside Press, Cambridge, 1880, p. 159.
2. The History of Our Country, by Abby Sage Richardson, Boston; Houghton, Osgood and Company, Riverside Press, Cambridge, 1880, p. 286.
3. Ibid.
4. Ibid.
5. Ibid, pp 286-287.
6. Complete Works of Abraham Lincoln, ed. John G. Nicolay and John Hay, 12 vols. New York; Francis D. Tandy Co. 1905, 1:43; pg. 8.
7. George Washington's vision, 1859, by Wesley Bradshaw – verbal account by Anthony Sherman a friend to President Washington.
8. Ibid.
9. Ibid.
10. The Constitution – A Glorious Standard; by President Ezra Taft Benson, Ensign, September 1987, pp 6-11.
11. Ibid.

Labans' Sword

Chapter **11**

About 600 B.C. the Lord commanded Lehi in a dream to take his family out of Jerusalem and depart into the wilderness. After packing necessary items and tents, Lehi's family traveled in secret by night from the city. Making their way by foot and camel, they soon reached the mountains (borders) just off the shoreline of the Red Sea. Entering the mountains, they set up a camp near a creek of water encircled within an extended valley hidden away from the sea.[1]

Shortly, thereafter, Lehi is blessed with a dream from the Lord commanding that his sons return to Jerusalem and obtain a record of the Jews. It was a record comparable to the Old Testament. It was a record of the Jews from Adam up to the time of Lehi's family. The record keeper was a man named Laban (a distant cousin of Lehi) containing a genealogy of Lehi's forefathers, and was engraven upon plates of brass.[2]

And it came to pass that I, Nephi, said unto my father: "I will go and do the things which the Lord hath commanded".[3] *And I, Nephi, and my brethren took our journey in the wilderness, with our tents, to go up to the Land of Jerusalem.*[4]

Reaching the outer walls of Jerusalem a decision was made: *And we cast lots – who of us should go in unto the house of Laban. And it came to pass that the lot fell upon Laman; and Laman went in unto the house of Laban.*[5]

Laban was angry, and thrust him out from his presence; and he would not that he should have the records.[6] Shortly, *We went down to the land of our inheritance, and we did gather together our gold, and our silver, and our precious things.*[7]

And after we had gathered these things together, we went up again unto the house of Laban. And it came to pass that we went in unto Laban, and desired him that he would give unto us the records which were engraven upon the plates of brass, for which we would give him our gold, and our silver, and all our precious things. And it came to pass that when Laban saw our property, and that it was exceedingly great, he did lust after it, insomuch that he thrust us out, and sent his servants to slay us, that he might obtain our property. And it came to pass that we did flee before the servants of Laban, and we were obliged to leave behind our property, and it fell into the hands of Laban.[8]

Nephi's brothers hid themselves while Nephi made a third attempt and crept back into the city making his way toward the house of Laban. Nephi stated: *And I was led by the spirit, not knowing beforehand the things which I should do. Nevertheless I went forth, and as I came near unto the house of Laban I beheld a man, and he had fallen to the earth before me, for he was drunken with wine. And when I came to him I found that it was Laban. And I beheld his sword, and I drew it forth from the sheath thereof; and the hilt thereof was of pure gold, and the workmanship thereof was exceedingly fine, and I saw that the blade thereof was of the most precious steel."*[9]

And it came to pass that I was constrained by the spirit that I should kill Laban; but I said in my heart: Never at any time have I shed the blood of man. And I shrunk and would that I might not slay him... And it came to pass that the spirit said unto me again: Slay him, for the Lord hath delivered him into thy hands... It is better that one man should perish rather than a nation should dwindle in unbelief... Therefore I did obey the voice of the spirit, and took Laban by the hair of the head, and I smote off his head with his own sword.[10]

Nephi obtained the brass plates and the sword of Laban then returns to his fathers' tent in the borders near the Red Sea. After a period of time Lehi receives another dream commanding him to send his sons back to Jerusalem to get Ishmael, a long time friend, and his family. Ishmael gathers up his family and items following Lehi's sons into the wilderness. Soon, thereafter, Lehi's and Ishmael's families leave the area starting a long journey across the Arabian Desert. Eight years later their final stop was in the land of Bountiful.[11]

While in Bountiful Nephi is commanded to build a ship to take the families to the Promised Land. *And it came to pass that after we had sailed for the space of many days we did arrive at the Promised Land; and we went forth upon the land and did pitch our tents; and we did call it the promised land.*[12]

And I, Nephi, had also brought the records which were engraved upon the plates of brass; and also the ball, or compass, which was prepared for my father by the hand of the Lord, according to that which is written.[13] *And I, Nephi, did take the sword of Laban, and after the manner of it did make many swords, lest by any means the people who were now called Lamanites should come upon us and destroy us.*[14]

After many years in America the family splits into two nations – the Nephites and the Lamanites. During this time Nephi carries with him the Sword of Laban, the plates of brass and other items and builds a temple after the manner of Solomon.[15]

Now Nephi began to be old, and he saw that he must soon die, wherefore he anointed a man to be a king and ruler over his people now, according to the reigns of the kings. The people having loved Nephi exceedingly, he having been a great protector for them, having wielded the sword of Laban in their defense, and having labored in all his days for their welfare.[16]

Wherefore, the people were desirous to retain in remembrance his name. And whoso should reign in his stead were called by the people, second Nephi, third Nephi, and so forth, according to the reigns of the kings.[17]

Fifty-five years had passed away from the time father Lehi left Jerusalem. Nephi gave Jacob, his younger brother, a commandment to write upon the golden plates a few of the things he considered to be most precious. Jacob, now the keeper of the records, followed the instruction of his older brother Nephi.[18]

Jacob began to be old and writes:... *Wherefore, I conclude this record, declaring that I have written according to the best of my knowledge, by saying that the time passed away with us, and also our lives passed away like as it were unto us a dream... And I, Jacob, saw that I must soon go down to my grave; wherefore, I said unto my son Enos: Take these plates. And I told him the things which my brother Nephi had commanded me, and he promised obedience unto the commands.*[19] Jacob bids farewell to his family securing the records, the Liahona and Laban's sword to the keeping of his son Enos.

Enos the grandson of Lehi and Sariah witnessed many wars between the Nephites and Lamanites in the course of his days. Now going on 179 years since Lehi left Jerusalem, Enos saw that he too must soon die.[20] So the record keeping goes to his son Jarom.

Jarom, a great-grandson to Lehi writes a small book about the Nephite nation's struggle in keeping the Lord's commandments. Jarom, as Keeper of Laban's Sword and the other relic's and records, notes that 200 years have passed away with the people of Nephi waxing strong in the land.[21]

Jumping ahead almost 985 years since Lehi and his family left Jerusalem, a prophet by the name of Mormon abridges their history onto the plates of Mormon. He speaks:... *I had made an abridgment from the plates of Nephi, down to the reign of this King Benjamin of whom Amaleki spake."*[22]

Wherefore, it came to pass that after Amaleki had delivered up these plates into the hands of King Benjamin, he took them and put them with the other plates, which contained records which had been handed down by the kings, from generation to generation until the days of King Benjamin.[23]

And it came to pass also that the armies of the Lamanites came down out of the land of Nephi, to battle against his people. But behold, King Benjamin gathered together his armies, and he did stand against them, and he did fight with the strength of his own arm, with the sword of Laban. And in the strength of the Lord they did contend against their enemies, until they had slain many thousands of the Lamanites.[24]

Around 34 A.D. the Americas were experiencing tempests, earthquakes, fires, whirlwinds and physical upheavals attesting to the crucifixion of Christ. Many, many people are destroyed. Darkness covered the land for three days and those who remain bemoaned their fate. *And many great and notable cities were sunk, and many were burned, and many were shaken till the buildings thereof had fallen to the earth, and the inhabitants thereof were slain, and the places were left desolate.*[25]

In the darkness the voice of Jesus Christ proclaims the destruction upon the Americas and their people. *Wo, wo, wo, unto this people; wo unto the inhabitants of the whole earth except they shall repent; for the devil laugheth, and his angels rejoice, because of the slain of the fair sons and daughters of my people; and it is because of their iniquity and abominations that they are fallen.*[26]

The darkness passed, the days passed and a great multitude of people gathered together round about the temple which was in the land Bountiful.[27] While conversing with each other, they heard a voice as if it came out of heaven and they cast their eyes round about.[28]

And behold, the third time they did understand the voice which they heard; and it said unto them: Behold my "Beloved Son", in whom I am well pleased, in whom I have glorified my name – hear ye him.[29]

They cast their eyes up again towards heaven; and behold, they saw a man descending out of heaven; and he was clothed in a white robe; and he came down and stood in the midst of them.[30]

Behold, I am Jesus Christ, whom the prophets testified shall come into the world.[31] *Arise and come forth unto me, that ye may thrust your hands into my side, and also that ye may feel the prints of the nails in my hands and in my feet, that ye may know that I am the God of Israel.*[32]

Moving ahead two hundred years since Christ's visit, the second generation had all passed away except a few.[33]

Around 305 A.D. *the people of Nephites and Lamanites had become exceedingly wicked one like unto another and the robbers of Gadianton did spread over all the face of the land. Amos died; and his brother, Ammoron, did keep the record in his stead. When three hundred and twenty years had passed away, Ammaron did hide up the records which were sacred – yea, even all the records which were sacred – yea, even all the sacred records, which had been handed down from generation to generation which were sacred.*[34]

About 322 A.D. Ammaron instructs Mormon concerning the sacred records. Mormon being about ten years of age is instructed: *When ye are about twenty and four years old go to the land Antum unto a hill which shall be called Shim; and there have I deposited unto the Lord all the sacred engravings concerning this people. Ye shall take the plates of Nephi unto yourself, and the remainder shall ye leave in the place where they are.*[35]

Several holy prophets over a time span of 1000 years (approximately 600 B.C. to 400 A.D.) held the Sword of Laban in defending freedom and liberty for their families; freedom upon the Americas for their wives and their children. The Sword of Laban is a holy sword just as is the Nauvoo Legion Sword belonging to Joseph Smith. Its symbolism is that of righteousness and freedom.

NOTES:

1. Book of Mormon, 1 Nephi 2:2-6
2. Book of Mormon, 2 Nephi 3:1-4
3. Book of Mormon, 1 Nephi 3:7
4. Book of Mormon, 1 Nephi 3:9
5. Book of Mormon, 1 Nephi 3:11
6. Book of Mormon, 1 Nephi 3:13
7. Book of Mormon, 1 Nephi 3:22
8. Book of Mormon, 1 Nephi 3:23-26
9. Book of Mormon, 1 Nephi 4:6-9
10. Book of Mormon, 1 Nephi 4:12-18
11. Book of Mormon, 1 Nephi 17:4-6
12. Book of Mormon 1 Nephi 18:23
13. Book of Mormon, 2 Nephi 5:12
14. Book of Mormon, 2 Nephi 5:14
15. Book of Mormon, 2 Nephi 5
16. Book of Mormon, Jacob 1:9-10
17. Book of Mormon, Jacob 1:11
18. Book of Mormon, Jacob 1
19. Book of Mormon, Jacob 7:26-27
20. Book of Mormon, Enos 1:25
21. Book of Mormon, Jarom 1:5
22. Book of Mormon, Words of Mormon 1:3
23. Book of Mormon, Words of Mormon 1:10
24. Book of Mormon, Words of Mormon 1:13-14
25. Book of Mormon, 3 Nephi 8:14
26. Book of Mormon, 3 Nephi 9:2
27. Book of Mormon, 3 Nephi 11:2
28. Book of Mormon, 3 Nephi 11:3
29. Book of Mormon, 3 Nephi 11:6-9
30. Book of Mormon, 3 Nephi 11:8
31. Book of Mormon, 3 Nephi 11:10
32. Book of Mormon, 3 Nephi 11:14
33. Book of Mormon, 4 Nephi 1:19-22
34. Book of Mormon, 4 Nephi 1:45-48
35. Book of Mormon, Mormon 1:2-4

Awake! O Ye People, The Savior is Coming

Chapter 12

Prince of Peace By: Lynne Millman-Weidinger See Appendix A

Around 6 B.C. a prophet by the name of Samuel the Lamanite came into the land of Zarahemla an ancient city in the Americas. He climbed upon a wall stretching forth his hand crying out with a loud voice prophesying unto the Nephite nation whatsoever things the Lord put into his heart.[1]

Even though Samuel the Lamanite was addressing the people of that day there is a certain pattern of warning to the people of our day. His voice rings out with clarity: ***"Prepare ye the way of the Lord".*** His voice is just a prelude to what lies ahead for us in our day. For in his day a great destruction fell upon the Americas and darkness covered the Promised Land.

The miracles of angels will never cease to minister unto the children of men. Our day is no different than the announcement of the birth of Christ[2] and His resurrection.[3]

An angel speaks out today through an LDS hymn written by William W. Phelps in the 1800's. It rings out: ***Awake! O Ye People, the Savior is coming*** *– today will soon pass and that unknown tomorrow may leave many souls in a more dreadful state than came by the flood, or that fell on Gomorrah. Yea, weeping and wailing when grief is too late.*[4]

And behold, the time cometh that he curseth your riches, that they become slippery, that ye cannot hold them, and in the days of your poverty ye cannot retain them.[5]

And in that day... *O that I had repented, and had not killed the prophets, - O that we had remembered the Lord our God in the day that he gave us our riches, and then they would not have become slippery that we should lose them; for behold, our riches are gone from us.*[6]

Behold, we lay a tool here and on the morrow it is gone; and behold, our swords are taken from us in the day we have sought them for battle.[7]

Samuel the Lamanite said: *And ye shall hear my words, for, for this intent have I come up upon the walls of this city, that ye might hear and know of the judgments of God which do await you because of your iniquities.*[8] Listen, open your eyes.

And in that day... things are becoming slippery just as it was in the evil days of the Nephites. *We are surrounded by demons, yea; we are* *encircled about by the angels of him who hath sought to destroy our souls.*[9] They are all about us day and night. Our earthly eyes being made of clay cannot see them, nevertheless our spirits can sense them all about us and war is waging upon us. It is a call to arms; put on the full armor of God. Our sword is FAITH, HOPE and CHARITY.

Picture Samuel the Lamanite standing on a wall looking upon them encircled with the Holy Ghost. Yet many Nephites did not believe in his words and became angry with him. They cast many stones and shot arrows at him but the spirit of the Lord was with him insomuch that they could not hit him with their stones neither with their arrows.[10]

And as they went forth to lay their hands on him, behold, he did cast himself down from the wall and did flee out of their lands.[11]

And in that day... just as in the day of the Nephites, scriptures are being fulfilled. Great signs and wonders are now given unto the people. Prophets and angels are declaring words of warning and miracles. Prepare ye the way of the Lord. The world, as we know it, will soon be burned and cleansed with fire. Yes, a Second Coming will be a "Global Warming". The polar ice caps will melt, oceans will shift, heavens and earth will shake, dry lands will appear, and, this earth as we know it, will become one land with few people. Just as Samuel the Lamanite warned the Nephite people, Joseph Smith and prophets in modern times send warnings to the inhabitants of earth to prepare to meet the Bridegroom our Savior Jesus Christ. The day is not far distant when the rainbow will lack its colors and 'global warming' will soon be upon us.

Samuel the Lamanite warned the Nephite people to expect tempests, earthquakes, fires, whirlwinds and physical upheavals to attest to the crucifixion of Christ. That day was just a prelude to the day of the Lord's return.

Samuel the Lamanite viewed the destruction upon the Americas. Darkness covered the land for three days with great destruction. A great storm such as one never known in all the land caused terrible thunder, shaking of the whole earth, and, sharp lightening. The city of Zarahemla was burned. The city of Moroni sunk into the depths of the sea. A great mountain arose in place of the city Moronihah.

Those who had not fallen could feel the vapor of the darkness. There was no light, neither torches, neither could there be fire kindled even with exceedingly dry wood. The mist of darkness was upon them. No light was seen and great were the groanings of the people.[12]

Highways were broken up, level roads were spoiled, many smooth places became rough, great cities sunk, many people were killed by the shaking of buildings. Some cities remained but the damage was extremely great. Many people were carried away in tornados. The whole earth was broken up into fragments.[13]

While in darkness and still of the night, a voice speaks out proclaiming a destruction of many people and cities for their wickedness:

"And many great destructions have I caused to come upon this land, and upon this people, because of their wickedness and their abominations."[14]

And in that day... the Lord said: *Yea, wo be unto the Gentiles except they repent; for it shall come to pass in that day, saith the Father, that I will cut off thy horses out of the midst of thee and I will destroy thy chariots.*[15] *And I will pluck up thy groves out of the midst of thee; so will I destroy thy cities.*[16]

The coming forth of the *Book of Mormon,* and the restoration of the complete gospel by the administration of angels is a sign that the Lord is commencing to gather Israel in fulfilling his covenants.

And ye may know that the words of the Lord, which have been spoken by the holy prophets, shall all be fulfilled; and ye need not say that the Lord delays his coming unto the children of Israel.[17]

And when ye shall see these sayings coming forth among you, then ye need not any longer spurn at the doings of the Lord, for the sword of his justice is in his right hand; and behold, at that day, if ye shall spurn at his doings he will cause that it shall soon overtake you.[18]

Yea, wo unto him that shall deny the revelations of the Lord, and that shall say the Lord no longer worketh by revelation, or by prophecy.[19]

Yea, and wo unto him that shall say at that day, to get gain, that there can be no miracle wrought by Jesus Christ.[20]

And now, we can behold the decrees of God concerning this land," (America) *"that it is a land of promise, and whatsoever nation shall possess it shall serve God, or they shall be swept off when the fullness of his wrath shall come upon them.*[21]

For behold, this is a land which is choice above all other lands; wherefore he that doth possess it shall serve God or shall be swept off; for it is the everlasting decree of God.[22]

NOTES:

1. Book of Mormon, Helaman 13:2-4
2. Book of Mormon, Moroni 7: 22, 25, 29
3. Book of Mormon, Helaman 13:34
4. Hymns of The Church of Jesus Christ of Latter-Day Saints, 1974, p. 183
5. Book of Mormon, Helaman 13:31
6. Book of Mormon, Helaman 13:33
7. Book of Mormon, Helaman 13:34
8. Book of Mormon, Helaman 14:11
9. Book of Mormon, Helaman 13:37
10. Book of Mormon, Helaman 16:2
11. Book of Mormon, Helaman 16:7
12. Book of Mormon, 3 Nephi 8:1-25
13. Book of Mormon, 3 Nephi 8:1-25
14. Book of Mormon, 3 Nephi 9:12
15. Book of Mormon, 3 Nephi 21:14
16. Book of Mormon, 3 Nephi 21:18
17. Book of Mormon, 3 Nephi 29:2
18. Book of Mormon, 3 Nephi 29:4
19. Book of Mormon, 3 Nephi 29:6
20. Book of Mormon, 3 Nephi 29:7
21. Book of Mormon, Ether 2:9
22. Book of Mormon, Ether 2:10

Moroni Prince Of America

Chapter 13

Around 400 A.D. an ancient prophet, Mormon, is witnessing the total destruction of his nation in a great battle surrounding the land of Cumorah. An immense battle is being fought upon this the American continent with hundreds of thousands slain by the sword.[1] The military engagement speaks out to the world by way of the *Book of Mormon.*

Moroni regarding his father Mormon said: *My father also was killed by them, and I even remain alone to write the sad tale of the destruction of my people. But behold, they are gone, and whether they will slay me, I know not.*[2]

And behold the Lamanites have hunted my people, the Nephites down from city to city and from place to place, even until they are no more; and great has been their fall; yea, great and marvelous is the destruction of my people, the Nephites.[3]

Mormon glancing into our day said: *Behold I speak unto you as though I spake from the dead, for I know that ye shall have my words.* [*Book of Mormon*][4] *I made this record out of the plates of Nephi, and hid up in the hill Cumorah all the records which had been entrusted to me by the hand of the Lord, save it were these few plates which I gave unto my son Moroni.*[5]

Moroni continues: *My father had made this record, and he hath written the intent thereof. And behold, I would write it also if I had room upon the plates, but I have not; and ore I have none, for I am alone. My father hath been slain in battle, and all my kinsfolk, and I have not friends nor wither to go; and how long the Lord will suffer that I may live I know not.*[6]

Behold I, Moroni, do finish the record of my father, Mormon. Behold, I have but few things to write, which things I have been commanded by my father.[7]

Referring to the *Book of Mormon* Moroni said: *Behold, I speak unto you as if ye were present, and yet ye are not. But behold, Jesus Christ hath shown you unto me, and I know your doings.*[8]

Yea, it shall come in a day when there shall be heard of fires, and tempests, and vapors of smoke in foreign lands; And there shall also be heard of wars, rumors of wars, and earthquakes in divers places. Yea, it shall come in a day when there shall be great pollutions upon the face of the earth; there shall be murders, and robbing, and lying, and deceivings, and whoredoms, and all manner of abominations.[9]

When men die as mortals, their bodies soon decay into Mother Earth and we too become angels. Men and women at times have special assignments from Heaven to visit loved ones in times of need or suffering. Mormon and his son Moroni passed from this earth and at times they also receive special heavenly assignments to visit the earth.

Mormon stated: *Or have angels ceased to appear unto the children of men? ...Behold I say unto you, Nay; it is by faith that angels appear and minister unto men.*[10] *Wherefore, by the ministering of angels, and by every word which proceeded forth out of the mouth of God, men began to exercise faith in Christ, they did lay hold upon every good thing; and thus it was until the coming of Christ.*[11]

July 4, 1854, a celebration was held at the Tabernacle in Salt Lake City, Utah. Elder Orson Hyde an Apostle addressed the people regarding the constitution of our country. The theme of his talk was centered upon an angel by the name of Moroni. He referred to him as the Guardian Angel of America.

The very name of America causes a thrill of patriotic devotion to her best interests to quiver in the heart of every citizen of Utah, with a zeal and a pride for the welfare of our country that does honor to the memory of those departed heroes whose ashes are mingled in our soil, and made rich and dear to us by their own blood.[12]

It was by the agency of that same angel of God that appeared unto Joseph Smith, and revealed to him the history of the early inhabitants of this country, whose mounds, bones, and remains of towns, cities, and fortifications speak from the dust in the ears of the living with the voice of undeniable truth.[13]

This same angel presides over the destinies of America, and feels a lively interest in all our doings. He was in the camp of Washington; and, by an invisible hand, led on our fathers to conquest and victory; and all this to open and prepare the way for the Church and the kingdom of God to be established on the Americas.[14]

In whatever land or country he perchance may roam – I mean the bold, manly, and daring act of our fathers in the Declaration of the Independence and Sovereignty of these United States – an act worthy to be engraven in letters of living light upon the tablets of our memory, and to be transmitted to our children, with the sacred charge that they teach it to their children, and to their children's children, till the "stripes and stars" float over every land, and are mirrored on the crest of every passing billow.[15]

This same angel was with Columbus, and gave him deep impressions, by dreams and by visions, respecting the New World. Under the guardianship of this same angel, or Prince of America, have the United States grown, increased, and flourished, like the sturdy oak by the rivers of water.[16]

And in that day regarding troubled times in our country he asserted: *But since the Prophets have been slain, the Saints persecuted, despoiled of their goods, banished from their homes, and no earthly arm to interpose for their rescue, what will be the future destiny of this highly-favored country? Should I tell the truth as it clearly passes before my mind's eye, my friends might censure me, and I might be regarded as an enemy to my country. If I should not tell the truth, but withhold it to please men, or to avoid giving offense to any, I might be regarded, by the powers celestial, as the enemy of God. What shall I do under these circumstances? Shall I be guilty of the crime of hesitating for a moment? No. Neither time nor place to hesitate now.*[17]

Speaking of his day: *In case of a general war, nation rising against nation, and kingdom against kingdom, which we have every reason to expect, it will be remembered that we have an extensive coast to defend, not only east and southerly, but also in the west. The transportation of troops will be unavoidable; and the sad and melancholy fate of many destined for the western coast by sea, around the southern cape, should admonish the Government to spare no pains or expense to construct a railroad with all dispatch across the continent, passing through the head and center of Utah Territory, particularly as the transportation of soldiers and munitions of war are among the less weighty reasons why a railroad should be constructed, connecting the Missouri River with the Pacific coast.*[18]

And in our day our U.S. boarders are no different with an extensive coast line to defend.

This angel "Prince of America" appeared to Joseph Smith in September 1823. Joseph was in the act of calling upon God when a personage appeared at his bedside. Joseph said: *He called me by name, and said unto me that he was a messenger sent from the presence of God to me, and that his name was Moroni; that God had a work for me to do.*[19] *He said there was a book deposited, written upon gold plates, giving an account of the former inhabitants of this continent and the source from whence they sprang.*[20]

The angel told of coming judgments by God soon upon the earth. He informed me of great judgments, with great desolations by famine, sword, and pestilence.[21]

He also said: For behold, the day cometh that shall burn as an oven, and all the proud, yea, and all that do wickedly shall burn as stubble; for they that come shall burn them, saith the Lord of Hosts, that it shall leave them neither root nor branch.[22]

Four years later, Joseph Smith receives the golden plates from Moroni, and, with the aid of the Urim and Thummim he translates the plates into the *Book of Mormon*. The scriptures is a history of the new world and teachings of God.

Oliver Cowdery proclaimed: *These were days never to be forgotten – to sit under the sound of a voice dictated by the inspiration of heaven, awakened the utmost gratitude of this bosom! Day after day I continued, uninterrupted, to write from his mouth, as he translated with the Urim and Thummim, or, as the Nephites would have said, 'Interpreters', the history or record called "The Book of Mormon".*[23]

Referring to the location of the gold plates, Joseph asserted: *Convenient to the village of Manchester, Ontario County, New York, stands a hill of considerable size. On the west side of this hill, not far from the top, under a stone of considerable size, lay the plates.*[24] *I made an attempt to take them out, but was forbidden by the messenger.*[25] Joseph met with

Moroni each year for four years thereafter before Moroni allowed him to receive the golden plates and start translation.

Catherine Salisbury, the oldest surviving sister of Joseph Smith, recorded in 1886: *I remember well the trials my brother had, before he obtained the records. After he had the vision, he went frequently to the hill, and upon returning he would tell us, "I have seen the records, also the brass plates and the sword of Laban with the breast plate and the interpreters".*[26]

A collection of sacred relics, the sword of Laban, and many plates of records were passed down through the centuries by the leaders of *Book of Mormon* history. The people viewed the sword of Laban as being a religious symbol and a sign of kingship and power. Nephi unsheathed the sword, as did King Benjamin, when warring against the Lamanite nation *"did fight with the strength of his own arm, with the sword of Laban".*[27] Thereafter the regalia was passed on and kept continuously.

The Lord echoed the words given by Alma to his son Helaman when speaking to Joseph Smith in 1829. He said, *"I have reserved those things which I have entrusted unto you, my servant Joseph, for a wise purpose in me, and it shall be made known unto future generations."* (D&C 5:9). He also promised that *"the testimony of three of my servants"* would be a witness to Joseph's testimony and that unto these three *"I will show these things"* (D&C 5:11) to the three witnesses Oliver Cowdery, David Whitmer and Martin Harris a promise was given by the Lord:[28] *"You shall have a view of the plates, and also of the breastplate, the sword of Laban, the Urim and Thummim, ... and the miraculous directors which were given to Lehi".*[29]

In the early days of the church many members knew about the Sword of Laban and looked upon it as an object of power with authority as elucidated in the *Book of Mormon.* It was a symbol of an ancient sword once held unsheathed by kings and prophets. Lt. General Joseph Smith, standing before the Nauvoo Legion as a military leader, unsheathed his sword and by doing so proved symbolic of the sword of Laban. The sword symbolized the strength of God's divine authority.

Moving ahead, on a bright sunny morning the 17th day of June 1877, a designated Stake Conference was held at the old Mormon Rock Chapel in Farmington, Davis County, Utah.[30] President Brigham Young joined by other church authorities are in attendance to create a new Davis Stake of Zion. The chapel is filled to capacity and consisted of many members of my family.

It is a special day for my great-grandfather William Reed Smith, his wife Eleanor Felshaw Smith and their four year old daughter Melvie. Eleanor was the fifth plural wife; she was not quite seventeen when she married William. Joseph Bates Noble was also in attendance and he was a close friend to Brigham Young and William Reed Smith.[31]

Brigham Young addressed the Conference and released Bishop William Reed Smith from his duties after serving 22 years in the Centerville Ward.

Christopher Layton, First Counselor — William Reed Smith, President — Anson Call, Second Counselor
First Davis Stake Presidency 1877-1882

After William is released as Bishop, he is appointed by President Young as President of the first Davis Stake with Christopher Layton and Anson Call as councilors. William Reed Smith served as Stake President for 17 years until his death on January 15, 1894.

On that day, Brigham gave a sermon about the treasures which the Lord has stored up in the earth. He related a story from the life of Oliver Cowdery. He prefaced his talk by saying, *"I tell these things to you, and I have a motive for doing so ... that they may grow to an understanding of some things that seem to be entirely hidden away from the human family... When Joseph got the plates, the angel instructed him to carry them back to the hill Cumorah, which he did. Oliver says that when Joseph and Oliver went there, the hill opened, and they walked into a cave, in which there was a large and spacious room. He says he did not think, at the time, whether they had the light of the sun or artificial light; but that it was just as light as day. They laid the plates on the table; it was a large table that stood in the room. Under this table there was a pile of plates as much as two feet high, and there were altogether in this room more plates than probably many wagon loads; they were piled up in the corners and along the walls. The first time they went there the sword of Laban hung upon the wall; but when they went there again it had been taken down and laid upon the table across the gold plates; it was unsheathed, and on it was written these words: "This sword will never be sheathed again until the kingdoms of this world become the kingdom of our God and his Christ."*[32]

Another time Brigham Young addressed the School of the Prophets (11 December 1869), he said: *"In relation to Joseph Smith returning the Plates of the Book of Mormon, that he did not return them to the box from whence he had received [them]. But he went [into] a cave in the Hill Cumorah with Oliver Cowdery, and deposited those plates upon a table or shelf. And in that room were deposited a large amount of gold plates containing sacred records. And when they first visited that room, the sword of Laban was hanging upon the wall, and when they last visited it, the sword was drawn from the scabbard and lain upon the table. And a messenger who was the keeper of the room informed them that the sword would never be returned to its scabbard until the Kingdom of God was established upon the Earth, and until it reigned triumphant over every enemy. Joseph Smith said that cave contained tons of choice treasures and records".*[33]

Then we have an account by William W. Phelps. Evidently it was shared by Hyrum Smith known as the earliest version. *"Joseph, Hyrum, Cowdery and Whitmer went to the Hill Cumorah. As they were walking up the hill, a door opened, and they walked into a room about 16 feet square. In that room was an angel and a trunk. On that trunk lay a Book of Mormon and gold plates, Laban's sword."*[34]

What was written on Laban's sword was a symbol of power, strength and divine authority. It served a righteous purpose for kings and prophets, and, at sometime, may be used by the Lord in bringing about his "righteous purposes unto the children of men" and "show forth his power unto future generations."[35]

NOTES:

1. Book of Mormon, Mormon 6.
2. Book of Mormon, Mormon 8:3.
3. Book of Mormon, Mormon 8:7.
4. Book of Mormon, Mormon 9:30.
5. Book of Mormon, Mormon 6:6.
6. Book of Mormon, Mormon 8:5.
7. Book of Mormon, Mormon 8:1.
8. Book of Mormon, Mormon 8:35.
9. Book of Mormon, Mormon 8:29-31.
10. Book of Mormon, Moroni 7:36-37
11. Book of Mormon, Moroni 7:25.
12. Celebration of the Fourth of July an address by Elder Orson Hyde, delivered in the Tabernacle, Great Salt Lake City, Utah, July 4, 1854, p. 368.
13. Ibid, p. 368.; and Celebration of the Fourth of July, by Orson Hyde (Journal of Discourses) vol. 6, pp. 367-3.
14. Ibid, p. 368; Ancient American Magazine (Wayne May, Editor) www.ancientamerican.com; Exploring The Book of Mormon in America's Heartland (Rod L. Meldrum, President; www.BookOfMormonEvidence.org).
15. Ibid, p. 367.
16. Ibid, p. 369.
17. Ibid, p. 369.
18. Ibid, p. 370.
19. Joseph Smith History, Chapter 1:27-33.
20. Ibid, Chapter 1:34.
21. Ibid, Chapter 1:45.
22. Ibid, Chapter 1:37.
23. Joseph Smith History – p. 58; Messenger and Advocate, Vol. 1 (October 1834). pp 14-16.
24. Joseph Smith History, Chapter 1:51.
25. Ibid, Chapter 1:53-54.
26. Katharine (Catherine) Salisbury, "Dear Sisters", The Saints Herald 33 (1 May 1886); 260 (emphasis added).
27. Book of Mormon, Words of Mormon 1:13.
28. Book of Mormon, Mosiah 28:11, 20; Alma 37: 1-2, 14;

Alma 50:38; 63:1, 11; 3 Nephi 1:1-2.

29. D&C 17:1.

30. Orson Pratt Brown – Life, Times Family, http://www.orsonprattbrown.com/Fife/christopher-layton.html.

31. Life and Times of Howard Carlos Smith, story of William Reed Smith by David F. Smith, p 94.

32. Journal of Discourses 19:38.

33. Dan Vogel, ed., Early Mormon Documents, Volume 3, Signature Books, SLC, UT; 2000, pp. 379-380, fn. 5; Quoted from Journal of Wilford Woodruff, LDS Church Archives, Spelling, punctuation and capitalization adjusted.

34. Ibid; quoted from Journal of William H. Dame, January 14, 1855, typescript, Special Collections, Harold B. Lee Library, BYU, Provo, UT.

35. D&C 17:3.

When The Earth Begins To Tremble

Chapter 14

John the Divine spoke of modern times – the day when a silence in Heaven is about to change. The half an hour is almost spent.[1]

An angel is now standing at the altar, having a golden censer with much incense. The smoke of the incense is the prayers of the Saints ascending up before God out of the angel's hand.[2]

And the angel took the censer and filled it with fire of the altar, and cast it into the earth: and there were voices and thunderings, and lightning, and an earthquake.[3]

President Gordon B. Hinckley delivered a warning of readiness at the October 2005 General Conference Priesthood Session:

I do not hesitate to say that this old world is no stranger to calamities and catastrophes. Those of us who read and believe the scriptures are aware of the warnings of prophets concerning catastrophes that have come to pass and are yet to come to pass.

How portentous are the words of revelation found in the 88th section of the Doctrine and Covenants concerning the calamities that should befall after the testimonies of the elders:

For after your testimony cometh the testimony of earthquakes, that shall cause groanings in the midst of her, and men shall fall upon the ground and shall not be able to stand.

And also cometh the testimony of the voice of thunderings, and the voice of lightnings, and the voice of tempests, and the voice of the waves of the sea heaving themselves beyond their bounds.

And all things shall be in commotion; and surely, men's hearts shall fail them; for fear shall come upon all people (D&C 88:89-91).

Someone has said it was not raining when Noah built the ark. But he built it, and the rains came.

The Lord has said, "If ye are prepared ye shall not fear" (D&C 38:30)

We can heed warnings. We are told by seismologists that the Salt Lake Valley is a potential earthquake zone. This is the primary reason that we are extensively renovating the Tabernacle on Temple Square. This historic and remarkable building must be made to withstand the shaking of the earth.

We have built grain storage and storehouses and stocked them with the necessities of life in the event of a disaster. But the best storehouse is the family storehouse. "Organize yourselves; prepare every needful thing."(D&C 109:8).

Our people for three-quarters of a century have been counseled and encouraged to make such preparations as will assure survival should a calamity come.

We can set aside some water, basic food, medicine, and clothing to keep us warm. We ought to have a little money laid aside in case of a rainy day.

We can so live that we can call upon the Lord for His protection and guidance. This is a first priority. We cannot expect His help if we are unwilling to keep his commandments.

The primary preparation is also set forth in the Doctrine and Covenants, where in it says, "Wherefore, stand ye in holy places, and be not moved, until the day of the Lord come." (D&C 87:8)[4]

In his talk, President Hinckley shares a song:

"When the earth begins to tremble

Bid our fearful thoughts be still;

When thy judgments spread destruction

Keep us safe on Zion's hill."

("Guide Us, O Thou Great Jehovah"

Hymns, 83)

Much more is spoken; however I'm going to end here. I recommend that you heed the Prophet's warning by reviewing his entire talk and reading the recommended scriptures.[5]

NOTES:

1. New Testament, Revelation 8:1.
2. New Testament, Revelation 8:3-4.
3. New Testament, Revelation 8:5.
4. Ensign, November 2005, President Gordon B. Hinckley, "If Ye Are Prepared, Ye Shall Not Fear".
5. Ibid.

Earthquake

Chapter 15

It is noteworthy for those who profess an interest in Bible scripture that God revealed many happenings concerning our time more than any other period in the history of mankind. Prophets of old have reached across centuries to warn us of upcoming events soon to be upon us.

A noted London palmist and seer "Cherio" having retired from individual practice (1934) compiled a book of "World Predictions". He made a statement, "Cheer up. The worst is yet to come". It was an article that came from the Deseret News, 1934. He speaks of a great inland sea and a new belt of land. His study is centered around planetary movements, precession of the equinoxes or the axis change of the earth.

He noted as time moves forward, a change is due. The equilibrium regarding the center of the earth will become altered and great earthquakes will take place in all parts of the world. This will cause severe earth tremors and quakes affecting countries which more or less have been immune from such occurrences. Extinct volcanoes around the earth will become active, and, tidal waves and cyclones will cause enormous destruction to property and cause death. This will continue until the earth's crust again becomes normal and settled.

He looks into the future: *An earthquake will develop northeasterly starting in the Pacific coast of Peru, passing through Panama, Mexico, United States, Canada and into the Arctic regions. New York, Washington, Boston, other eastern cities, and Toronto will be seriously affected and a considerable part of New York will be destroyed.*[1]

Things may change, and a shaking could cause the ocean to break up the Isthmas of Panama. On the other hand the Sahara Desert omnifacial could be transformed into a great inland sea and the temperate zone of Palestine, Egypt and surrounding countries becoming a great center of civilization.[2]

A new ridge of land will appear in the North Atlantic, diverting the Gulf Stream so that cold will increase in the northeastern states of America, affecting similarly Ireland, Great Britain, Sweden, Norway, Denmark, the northern parts of Russia and Germany, and also France and Spain.[3]

Thus, a new highway will be cast upon a ridge of land: *And they who are in the north countries shall come in remembrance before the Lord; and their prophets shall hear his voice, and shall no longer stay themselves; and they shall smite the rocks, and the ice shall flow down at their presence.*[4]

The Lord stated: *Behold, I sent you out to testify and warn the people, and it becometh every man who hath been warned to warn his neighbor.*[5]

For after your testimony cometh the testimony of earthquakes, that shall cause groaning in the mist of her, and men shall fall upon the ground and shall not be able to stand.

And the voice of tempests and the voice of the waves of the sea heaving themselves beyond their bounds. And all things shall be in commotion; and surely, men's hearts shall fail them, for fear shall come upon all people.[6]

Your old men shall have dreams, your young men shall see visions.[7] *Alas for the day! for the day of the Lord is at hand, and as a destruction from the almighty shall it come.*[8]

Earthquake

One early morning a wake up call came to me. It was so real that I must share it as a warning.

Suddenly I was on the upper deck looking in all directions covering most of southern Idaho. It seemed like a summer day. It was calm with no wind. People were working, some were playing and others tended to their gardens.

Without warning the ground started to shake with a thunderous noise rolling like waves of the sea. I reached out to brace myself on the railing. The floor joists and ceiling rafters were creaking very loudly, I could hardly stand. What is happening?

As my view opened up I was able to see houses, garages, barns, power poles, shrubbery and trees swaying extensively back and forth. All was in motion, and it seemed never ending. It seemed as though the motion continued for several minutes. As I watched the swaying, there appeared a protective shield of some sort outlining Cassia County and the surrounding areas. I witnessed no houses or structures falling to the ground.

After the severity of the shaking I suddenly found myself inside a house of an elderly widow. She was crying and very upset but seemed uninjured. She said, "I don't want to live, I want to die. My house is in ruins, the walls are cracked and floors are uneven. Pictures are off the walls and glass is everywhere." I told her, "Don't worry, your house is still standing. It weathered the earthquake and is restorable. You're greatly blessed." A peace came upon her, and she was calm. A feeling came upon me that many cities of our great country did not weather so well especially the eastern coast.

Brigham Young: *Save all pins, needles, buttons, buckles, nails, leather, pieces of cloth and rags, because the day will come when it will be almost impossible to secure them. Save your crusts and dry bread, delicious puddings can be made from them; save bacon rinds, tallow, and grease for making soap. Do not waste anything, for the time will come when it will be hard to get these things, and they will be greatly needed.*[9]

It might be wise to take an inventory for a sudden unexpected emergency situation such as an earthquake. Lack of food, water, heat, bedding, clothing and other items may be hard to come by. Prepare, don't be caught lacking.

NOTES:

1. Cherio's Predictions – from Deseret News, 1934.
2. Ibid.
3. Ibid.
4. D&C 133:26-27.
5. D&C 88:81.
6. D&C 88:89-91.
7. Old Testament, Joel 2:28.
8. Old Testament, Joel 1:15.
9. Advice given to the Saints in Provo, Utah by President Brigham Young and recorded in the diary of Ben H. Bullock of Provo, Utah 1901.

Just My Lucky Day Chapter 16

A friend beyond this world *Ezra Taft Benson* was born August 4, 1899 in Whitney Idaho, the son of George T. Benson, Jr. and Sarah Dunkley Benson. He was the first of eleven children. I say a friend even though our paths did not cross in this life other than me listening to him speak as an General Authority and President of the Church. I read all his books, talks and listened intensely whenever he addressed the members of the church.

I remember visiting the Deseret Industries on Main Street in Salt Lake City. It was a late Saturday afternoon in the spring of 1994. It was a dismal day with threatening rain and clouds covering the valley. Unbeknownst to me, President Ezra Taft Benson was nearing death.

Being down in spirit, my main objective was to purchase an antique picture frame to cover a puzzle picture of a lighthouse.

Walking about the store looking for a bargain or two, I asked an employee the whereabouts for a picture frame. She pointed to a corner section of the store. Following her directions I made my way between the racks to an area of discarded frames; some were sitting on display shelves looking a bit ragged in need of repair. None met my eye. She then directed me to another corner of the building where more picture frames were stacked in disarray.

Going unnoticed I looked through a stack of many dusty frames several feet high appearing as if they were placed there a long time ago. Each picture frame, of assorted sizes, lacked a picture. I uncovered one at a time carefully shaking off a cloud of dust. Reaching near the end of the stack, I felt a spirit upon me saying "don't stop;" I listened to the small voice and I carefully removed one at a time until I reached the bottom of the pile. Only one picture frame left – time for a break.

As I head toward the men's room to wash my hands, I wonder "why am I here?" I could be spending my Saturday doing something fun like a movie, fishing, or just hanging out in the comfort of my home. Returning to the corner I picked up the last remaining frame from off the floor, carefully shaking away the dust. Turning it around I quickly noticed a painting within the frame. Suddenly an electric shock passed across my hands.

Before my eyes appeared a portrait of President Ezra Taft Benson. What a prize! How did it end up here in this dusty pile? Where did it hang before being donated, and who in the world would discard an oil painting of a living prophet? With my heart pounding, I quickly made my way to the cashier.

Waiting in line to cash out, several people asked where I found such a unique portrait of the Prophet. I just smiled saying "It was quite accidental" or "Just my lucky day". Picking up the picture, a woman cashier commented, "This is an unusual portrait, where did you find it?" I said, "Over in the discarded picture frame section". She responded, "How can that be? It is such an awesome gift. I didn't know it was there." The register rang my tab and to my surprise a "Prophet's Portrait" was only $3.00.

Currently it is 4:00 a.m., and I am sitting at the kitchen table writing this chapter. Comparing the picture portrait of President Benson to his funeral service program I notice something quite unique. The picture selected for the funeral program is the same as the portrait. I understand why the electric shock went across my hands.

Back to a raining day in 1994, I return home sharing my experience and prize with my wife and daughters (Heather and Catrina). They could hardly believe that I found a picture frame with an oil painting of the Prophet. Conference weekend was coming soon, and we planned on spending time at Yuba Lake in our aged motor home. We planned on watching conference from a newly purchased battery operated portable television. Things didn't go well that weekend. It rained and rained, and we could not receive television transmission. Nevertheless we were able to listen to conference on the radio.

A Prophets' Visit

Chapter 17

Tuesday May 31, 1994 Deseret News wrote an article regarding the death of President Ezra Taft Benson:

Deseret News – Tuesday, May 31, 1994

President Ezra Taft Benson who served the Church of Jesus Christ of Latter-day Saints as church president and general authority for more than 50 years, died Monday at 2:35 p.m. at his home of congestive heart failure. He was 94.

The church's 13th president, President Benson had been in frail health during his last years. He last spoke in general conference in October 1989. He attended several sessions since then but did not speak. His last public appearance was at his wife's funeral nearly two years ago.[1]

Catrina, our youngest daughter, has always felt a spiritual connection with our church leaders. Since age 6 she has written many letters to the presidents and apostles. No less than six letters to President Ezra Taft Benson with two return letters bearing his signature. President Benson was too sick to sign the other letters however he answered them by way of his secretary.

On the night of President Benson's death, I experienced a dream in an early morning hour. It was very real and special.

I found myself inside an old red brick house dated in the early 1900's. I was in a rocking chair within a living room rocking. I could view a side kitchen with my wife putting the finishing touches onto Sunday dinner stirring the roast beef gravy.

Rocking back and forth, I couldn't help but notice the antique furniture which included hanging lights, flower wallpaper, pictures with golden frames, and a standing lamp with a fancy shade top. It was a beautiful room to behold with colorful braided floor rugs, white base molding bordering the ceiling and floor edge. Family pictures lined the mantle while a large fireplace warmed the room. It was very peaceful.

Suddenly a tap-tap-tap on the front door, and I was up off the rocker making my way toward the large door. I couldn't help but notice a bright light reflecting under the door. It was a colorful display encircling the entry.

Opening the door I was in awe to see President Ezra Taft Benson and his wife Flora. They stood tall hand in hand with glowing smiles. Each dressed in white, President Benson wore a suit and tie while Sister Benson wore a long laced dress. Each had a glow of whiteness beyond earthly description. Looking young in spirit and body, it was almost like a date – they were so happy.

I was stunned wondering why they were visiting our home. President Benson greeted me asking, "If we might visit for a moment." Of course, the answer was "Yes". He was like a father figure being very relaxed, smiling as he looked upon me.

He stated, "My main purpose is to visit with your daughter Catrina, is she here?" I said "yes" immediately asking my wife to get Catrina. While waiting, I asked President Benson his opinion regarding my aging father. He is 88 years old and sick upon his bed. He stated, "You don't need to worry about your father for he is just a young man." He then smiled, embraced me and whispered into my ear saying, "I love your family. It's time to leave."

After Jolene woke, I talked with her regarding my dream. Morning was moving on, so we thought it best to check on Catrina. She was sleeping later than usual and was difficult to awaken. She too was visited by President Benson. Listening intently, it was apparent that she had visited the upper room of the Salt Lake Temple. Her visit is recorded in our family history and is very sacred. I know that she had been in this upper room as I had the opportunity to attend a meeting in that room as a newly returned missionary.

President Thomas S. Monson in addressing the saints in the Conference Session 3 April 1993 shared an occasion with President Benson:

President Benson instructed us: "Sometimes in the peace of lovely temples, the serious problems of life find their solutions. [At times] pure knowledge flows to us there under the influence of the Spirit . . . temples really are the gateways to heaven."

President Monson again referenced President Benson while at the Denver Colorado Temple dedication:

He said: May we remember always, as we [visit and work in these glorious temples], that the veil may become very thin between this world and the spirit world. I know this is true." He declared, "It is well also that we keep in mind that it is all one great program on both sides of the veil and it is not too important whether we serve here or over there, as long as we serve with all our heart, might, mind and strength.[2]

Preparing to return home after serving a two-year LDS mission, Elder Benson sent a letter to Flora Smith Amussen, a girl he had dated before his mission, and asked her to marry him. She replied she would first like to serve her own mission. She served in the Hawaiian Mission, then returned home and married Ezra.

Sister Flora Amussen as a missionary experienced a locked temple door. President Benson shares:

She had been officiating part time in the (Hawaii) Temple while on her mission, and this particular night the session had run a bit late, and she had been delayed for some reason. So when she got to the door she found that it was locked. She was in and everyone else had gone, and she was alone in the temple. The mission home in those days was situated across a stile, over a fence, and through some trees.

When she found she was locked in, she tried the door and said, 'Yes, I can open it from the inside.' But she said a prayer that she would be protected, because in those days there was a camp in the trees just off the trail to the mission home, and there had been some incidents, so she was worried. She prayed to the Lord that she would be protected, and then she started toward the door.

As she stepped outside the door, there was a circle of light all around her person, and that circle of light accompanied her all the way to the mission home – over the stile, through the trees, to the door of the mission home.[3]

In a talk by President Spencer W. Kimball on April 1974 he said: *The Lord has revealed to men by dreams some-think more than I ever understood or felt before. I heard this more than once in quorum meetings of the Council of the Twelve when George F. Richards was president.*

I believe in dreams, brethren. The Lord has give me dreams which to me are just as real and as much from God as when Lehi so through a dream led his colony out of the old country across the mighty deep to this promised land, or any other dreams that we might read in the scripture...

It is not out of place for us to have important dreams. Forty years ago I had a dream which I am sure was from the Lord. In this dream I was in the presence of my Savior as he stood mid-air. He spoke no word to me, but my love for him was such that I have not words to explain. I know that no mortal man can love the Lord as I experienced that love for the Savior unless God reveals it to him. I would have remained in his presence but there was a power drawing me away from him.[4]

President Benson loved children. He is well remembered for singing "A Mormon Boy" with a group of children on a video tape aired at the conclusion of the April 1989 conference at the Salt Lake Tabernacle.

NOTES:

1. Deseret News Tuesday May 31, 1994 – No. 351 – President Benson dies at 94 of heart failure. Front page.
2. "Temple Memories", address given at Denver Colorado Temple dedication, 25 Oct 1986.
3. President Benson emulated missionary examples of Family members. Deseret News, May 31, 1994, p 3.
4. The Cause is Just and Worthy, by President Spencer W. Kimball, The Ensign, May 1974, p 119.

Blow Ye The Trumpet

Chapter 18

A prophecy is like a thin thread of scripture covering the creation to the ends of time. It seems to interweave itself with each other into a mat of interlaced scripture covering each dispensation. It's a warning voice collectively speaking from their time into our time. It's like a dream passing you by unless you have a listening ear. If the ear is waxed you may not hear and the warning may pass you by.

When a prophet speaks, look forward as prophecy encircles us in all directions. Prophecy is a miracle of events. It surrounds you with advice, directions and warnings.

Nearly 2,800 years ago the Prophet Joel spoke with a voice ringing loud and clear into our day.

Alas for the day! for the day of the Lord is at hand, and as a destruction from the Almighty shall it come.[1]

Hear this, ye old men, and give ear, all ye inhabitants of the land. Hath this been in your days, or even in the days of your father? Tell ye your children of it, and let your children tell their children, and their children another generation.[2]

Blow ye the trumpet in Zion, and sound an alarm in my holy mountain: let all the inhabitants of the land tremble: for the day of the Lord cometh, for it is nigh at hand.[3]

We live in the 'evil of times' and it should be written. When the great city of New York and other cities are no longer, they will read and look back into our time with amazement and wonderment. We will be looked upon as the pioneers of our time by sharing our histories.

A prophet by the name of Malachi spoke to his people in and around Jerusalem. He sent a reproof among the people as to their evil practices. He also had visions many years into the future and on into our day. He spoke of a messenger to prepare the way of the Lord.

Behold, I will send my messenger, and he shall prepare the way before me: and the Lord, whom ye seek, shall suddenly come to his temple.[4]

The Prophet Daniel in his writings during the Babylonian captivity envisioned a latter day prophet restoring the true church: *And in the days of these kings shall the God of heaven set up a kingdom, which shall never be destroyed: and the kingdom shall not be left to other people, but it shall break in pieces and consume all these kingdoms, and it shall stand for ever.*[5]

The Lord has given warning through the ancient and modern prophets: *Wherefore, I the Lord, knowing the calamity which should come upon the inhabitants of the earth, called upon my servant Joseph Smith, Jun., and spake unto him from heaven, and gave him commandments.*[6]

And it shall come to pass that he that feareth me shall be looking forth for the great day of the Lord to come, even for the signs of the coming of the Son of Man.[7]

And there shall be earthquakes also in divers places, and many desolations; yet men will harden their hearts against me, and they will take up the sword, one against another, and they will kill one another.[8]

And they shall see signs and wonders, for they shall be shown forth in the heavens above, and in the earth beneath.[9]

Wherefore, stand ye in holy places, and be not moved, until the day of the Lord come; for behold, it cometh quickly, saith the Lord."[10]

Wherefore the voice of the Lord is unto the ends of the earth, that all that will hear may hear.[11]

Prepare ye, prepare ye for that which is to come, for the Lord is nigh. And the anger of the Lord is kindled, and his sword is bathed in heaven, and it shall fall upon the inhabitants of the earth."[12]

And thus, with the sword and by bloodshed the inhabitants of the earth shall mourn; and with famine, and plague, and earthquake, and the thunder of heaven, and the fierce and vivid lightning also, shall the inhabitants of the earth be made to feel the wrath, and indignation, and chastening hand of an Almighty God, until the consumption decreed hath made a full end of all nations.[13]

Wherefore, O ye Gentiles, it is wisdom in God that these things should be shown unto you, that thereby ye may repent of your sins, and suffer not that these murderous combinations shall get above you, which are built up to get power and gain – and the work, yea, even the work of destruction come upon you, yea, even the sword of the justice of the Eternal God shall fall upon you to your overthrow and destruction if ye shall suffer these things to be.[14]

For it cometh to pass that whoso buildeth it up seeketh to overthrow the freedom of all lands, nations, and countries; and it bringeth to pass the destruction of all people, for it is built up by the devil, who is the father of all lies.[15]

Behold, the sword of vengeance hangeth over you; and the time soon cometh that he avengeth the blood of the saints upon you, for he will not suffer their cries any longer.[16]

Behold I say unto you, he that denieth these things knoweth not the gospel of Christ; yea, he has not read the scriptures; if so, he does not understand them.[17]

Yea, it shall come in a day when the power of God shall be denied, and churches become defiled and be lifted up in the pride of their hearts. Yea, it shall come in a day when there shall be heard of fires, and tempests, and vapors of smoke in foreign lands. And there shall also be heard of wars, rumors of wars, and earthquakes in divers places. Yea, it shall come in a day when there shall be great pollutions upon the face of the earth; there shall be murders, and robbings, and lying, and deceivings, and whoredoms, and all manner of admonitions.[18]

Behold, I am God; give heed unto my word, which is quick and powerful, sharper than a two edged sword, to the dividing asunder of both joints and marrow; therefore give heed unto my words.[19]

NOTES:

1. Holy Bible, Joel 1:15.
2. Holy Bible, Joel 1:2-3.
3. Holy Bible, Joel 2:1.
4. Holy Bible, Malachi 3:1.
5. Holy Bible, Daniel 2:44.
6. D&C 1:17.
7. D&C 45:39.
8. D&C 45:33.
9. D&C 45:40.
10. D&C 87:8.
11. D&C 1:11.
12. D&C 12:13.
13. D&C 87:6.
14. Book of Mormon, Ether 8:23.
15. Book of Mormon, Ether 8:25.
16. Book of Mormon, Mormon 8:41.
17. Book of Mormon, Mormon 9:8.
18. Book of Mormon, Mormon 8:28-31.
19. D&C 6:2.

A Test Is Upon Us Chapter 19

In the twinkling of an eye, thirty-seven years have passed since my friend, LaRell J. Hatch, exited into another world. It was very sudden and he was caught by surprise.

At the time I was a second councilor in our ward bishopric and LaRell served as our Bishop. Just a little about him: his wife Jackie was always at his side, they have five children, he taught elementary school, he served a two year LDS mission to New Zealand and graduated from Brigham Young University.

The High Priest Quorum voted to build a hay barn for a family as a Ward building project. The barn cement footings were laid in late September 1974. By early December, we had completed a greater part of the walls and in the process of laying plywood on the roof. The roof had a slight slope. Someone could walk quite easily on the roof without a fear of falling.

Bishop Hatch and I spent one sunny afternoon completing the west wall. We joked with each other as to who could work the fastest. He could out nail me every time. He did the same thing in hoeing sugar beets at the church farm. The Bishop could hoe two rows to my one. Many times LaRell expressed a great love for his family, the gospel and people with whom he labored within the mission field. He showed a deep love for the scriptures as witnessed by underlined verses with many worn pages. They were scriptures that gave special meaning to his life.

We were asked as a High Priest Quorum to work a few hours on New Years Day. As one worker cut a hole for a skylight, a circular saw suddenly came unplugged. He reached around to re-plug the cord, just as Bishop Hatch walked onto the skylight plywood. He broke through falling downward onto the frozen ground. A member who witnessed the fall from below stated LaRell fell straight through the rafters feet first then halfway down he completely turned landing squarely on the lower part of his neck and back.

Several weeks later after his passing, we voted as a Ward High Priest Quorum to return and complete the project. Many dreams, visions and other sacred happenings took place during this time span.

Shortly after his death, I had a visit which was very real and added special meaning to my life. I was standing in the main foyer of a South Jordan Wardhouse. Sacrament meeting had just ended, and members quietly mingled with each other. My mind at that time was reflecting upon the passing of LaRell. My eyes were suddenly centered upon the south entrance into the church. I saw LaRell walking hurriedly up the sidewalk through the glass entrance into the church foyer. I cannot express my joy in seeing him. He was dressed in a dark suit carrying a brown envelope in his hand. His eyes were full of spiritual knowledge. His face carried no smile. I felt quite hurt as he seemed to be in such a hurry walking right past me. He then tapped the new Bishop of our Ward on the shoulder who was talking with several members and didn't notice LaRell. LaRell was completely unnoticed in the foyer. He made several attempts to talk with the two new councilors but had no success. He again tried to talk with the Bishop but without success.

He then hurriedly walked over to where I was standing and took from the brown envelope several checks, paper money and loose change. He gave the money and checks to a sister standing next to me. He talked with her briefly asking her to give the tithing money to her Bishop. I was unable to identify the sister as my complete attention was centered upon LaRell. He was full of the Spirit of the Lord, and his eyes carried such added spiritual knowledge. His face showed an expression of concern and longing to stay. He made no attempt to shake hands, only to deliver his message. He then turned to me and made the following statement, *"Howard, no one in the foyer has noticed my presence except you and this sister."* His face then saddened and he stated, *"I will not have to go through the hard times that are about to fall upon the saints. These times will shortly be upon this people and only the strong in faith will survive the TEST."*

LaRell then hurriedly passed through the south glass exit of the church. I called out, "Bishop Hatch, please come back, don't leave now." He looked over his shoulder and he gave me a LOOK of understanding as if to say "We will meet again in the hereafter." I knew this would be the last time I would see him in this life. As soon as LaRell left the building, tears flowed down my cheeks.

Circling Fortress

Chapter 20

President Edward J. Wood of the Cardston Temple talked about a woman who visited the temple before its dedication; several weeks later she wrote from her home about some of her impressions. I would like to share several of her comments. Keep in mind we're traveling back many years. This woman visited the temple some nineteen years before World War II. It's interesting to see how her reflections intertwine to this time of the world.

Her remarks remind me of an old picture frame. She is the centerpiece looking out from within the picture into our time and further on into another time. I get the feeling her reflection is closing upon us and not too far into the distant future.

She said: *There is a place called Cardston. It was once a modern town. A temple linking the past with the future has now been built in Cardston, and the town has now become a collection of flimsy huts, nestling at the feet of the temple. These will soon pass away into oblivion, but the temple will continue to function for the spiritual purposes for which it was raised. Inside the temple it seemed as though the temple was filled with actual spiritual bodies of these previous leaders of your church, each seeming to have the work that person was engaged in whilst in the flesh. I saw persons who were leaders of your church, during its march across the American desert, now engaged in helping these higher patriarchs under whose orders they seemed to be working. It was these latter spiritual leaders, if I may use that term, who seemed to be instructed to show me the scenes here recorded.*[1]

My exterior impression of the building was that of a place of waiting for a higher civilization than our present one.

I saw Cardston and the surrounding foothills, especially north and west, for miles, being prepared as a refuge for your people quietly but quickly.

I saw Elders still under divine guidance, counseling and encouraging the planting of every available acre of soil in this district, so that large supplies would be near the refuge.

I saw artesian wells and other wells dug all over that territory so that when the open waters were polluted and poisoned that the people of the church and their cattle should be provided for.

I saw the fuel resources of the district develop in many places with vast piles of coal and timber stored for future use and buildings.

I saw provisions made for a big influx of people who will not at first belong to the church, but who will gather in their tribulation. The territory will be carefully surveyed and mapped out for the camping of this great body of people.

I saw vast quantities of surgical appliances, medicines, disinfectants, etc. stored in the temple basement.

I saw defensive preparation working out the organizations of the camps on maps.

I saw the nursing corridors used as places of storage underground.

I saw the hills surveyed and corrals built in sequestered places for cattle, sheep, etc., quickly and quietly.[2]

Let's reflect back and look at several prophecies given by Brigham Young.

When the testimony of the Elders ceases to be given; and the Lord says to them, "Come home; I will preach my own sermons to the nations of the earth. The sermon will be preached with fire and sword, tempests, earthquakes, hail, rain, thunders and lightening, and fearful destruction. You will hear of magnificent cities, idolized by the people, sinking in the earth, entombing the inhabitants.[3]

The Sea will heave itself beyond its bounds, engulfing mighty cities.

Famine will spread over the nations and nation will rise up against nation.

Kingdom against kingdom and state against state in our own country and in foreign lands; and they will destroy each other, caring not for the blood and lives of their neighbors, of their families, nor of their own lives.[4]

The temple lady goes on to say: *I saw chaos developed in its varying stages, faction against faction, nation against nation.*

I saw all in open or secret hostility to your people and your faith.

I saw your people draw closer and closer together, as this became more tense.

I saw spiritual forces warn them through the mouth of your elders and your other officers.

I saw the spiritual forces influencing those members who had drifted away, to re-enter the fold.

I saw greater tithing than ever before.

I saw vast quantities of necessities supplied by members who spiritual eyes had been opened.

I saw a liquidation of properties and effects disposed of quietly but quickly by members of the church, as the spirits influence directed them.

I saw the inspired call sent forth to all the church, to gather to the refuges of Zion.

I saw the stream of your people quietly moving in the direction of their refuge.

I saw your people moving more quickly and in larger numbers until all the stragglers were housed.

I saw the wireless message flashed from Zion's refuge to Zion's refuge in their several places that all was well with them.

I then saw darkness of chaos closed around the boundaries of your people.

I saw the last days of tribulation had begun.[5]

Just how close are we? What will I do today if I am brave? I will follow the counsel of our church leaders. Quoting one of my favorite scriptures Amos 3:7, *Surely the Lord God will do nothing, but he revealeth his secret unto his servants the prophets.*[6]

Elder L. Tom Perry said: ***I believe it is time, and perhaps with some urgency, to review the counsel we have received in dealing with our personal and family preparedness...*** *We have been instructed to follow at least four requirements in preparing for that which is to come. Gain an adequate education, Live within your income, Avoid unnecessary debt, Store a reserve of food and supplies...* ***As long as I can remember, we have been taught to prepare for the future and to obtain a years supply of necessities.*** *I would guess that the years of plenty have almost universally caused us to set aside this counsel. I believe the time to disregard this counsel is over.* ***With events in the world today, it must be considered with all seriousness.***[7]

President Gordon B. Hinckley counseling on becoming self reliant: *Now brethren, I want to make it very clear that I am not prophesying, that I am not predicting* ***years*** *of famine in the future.* ***But, I am suggesting that the time has come to get our houses in order...There is a portent of stormy weather ahead to which we had better give heed...We are carrying a message of self-reliance throughout the church... I urge you brethren to look to the condition of your finances... May the Lord bless you, my beloved brethren, to set your houses in order...That's all I have to say about it, but I wish to say it with all the emphasis of which I am capable.***[8]

Several key things should be remembered in preparing for the events now upon us. We have been told repeatedly to prepare by putting aside food storage, water, and emergency essentials. We have been told to learn how to garden, cook, sew, and preserve food as well as learning to get along on less money. We are to prepare ourselves spiritually. We need not fear if we follow the admonitions of our church leaders, keep the commandments, separate ourselves from the things of the world and keep a pathway open to the temple.

Sometimes we bask in our own comfortable complacency rationalizing that the ravages of war, economic disaster, famine, and earthquakes on a large scale cannot happen here. Some who believe this are not acquainted with the revelations of the Lord. It can happen here.

NOTES:

1. The Last Days by Robert W. Smith, 6th Edition, July, 1943, pp 49-58. Temple President Edward J. Wood Shared a talk with a visitor.
2. The Last Days by Robert W. Smith, 6th Edition, July 1943. pp 49-58.
3. Brigham Young, Journal of Discourses, Vol. 10, p 73.
4. Brigham Young, Journal of Discourses, Vol 10, p 295.
5. The Last Days by Robert W. Smith, 6th Edition, July, 1943, pp 49-58. Temple President Edward J. Wood Shared a talk with a visitor.
6. Old Testament, Amos 3:7.
7. Elder L. Tom Perry, General Conference, Oct 1975.
8. President Gordon B. Hinckley, General Conference, October 1998, Priesthood Session.

Brightness Of His Coming

Chapter 21

A warning to the people in our time by the Lord through His prophets: *Prepare ye, prepare ye for that which is to come, for the Lord is nigh; And the anger of the Lord is kindled, and his sword is bathed in heaven, and it shall fall upon the inhabitants of the earth.*[1]

In December 1962 Elder Benson gave this warning: *We as a people have never known bondage. Liberty has always been our blessed lot. Few of us have ever seen people who lost their freedom – their liberty. And when reminded of the danger of losing our liberty and independence our attitude has usually been, 'It can not happen here'. We have become lulled away into a false security.*[2]

December 1965 a warning by President David O. McKay: *Freedom of choice is more to be treasured than any other possession earth can give. Whether born in abject poverty or shackled at birth by inherited riches, every one has the most precious of all life's endowments – the Gift of Free Agency, man's inherited and inalienable right.*[3]

We must remember that man is superior over government. It should not be the other way. Government is nothing more than a relatively small group of citizens who have been hired by the people to perform certain functions and discharge certain responsibilities which have been authorized by us – the people.

President Joseph Fielding Smith also gives a most timely message even though it is now many years later. *Now I tell you it is time the people of the United States were waking up with the understanding that if they don't save the constitution from the dangers that threaten it, we will have a change of government.*[4]

In June 1966 Elder Ezra Taft Benson said: *The only limitation on you and me is within ourselves. That we will develop the understanding, the desire, and the courage, born of the Spirit, to eschew socialism and to support and sustain, in the manner revealed and as interpreted by the Lord, those just and holy principles embodied in the Constitution of the United*

States for the protection of all flesh, in the exercise of their God – given agency.[5]

President J. Reuben Clark warned us: We *stand in danger of losing our liberties, and that once lost, only blood will bring them back; and once lost, we of this church will, in order to keep the Church going forward, have more sacrifices to make and more persecutions to endure than we have yet known . . .*[6]

In the April 1965 Conference Elder Ezra Taft Benson added this warning: *Brethren, if we had done our homework and were faithful, we could step forward at this time and help save this country. The fact that most of us are unprepared to do it is our indictment we will have to bear. The longer we wait, the heavier the chains, the deeper the blood, the more the persecution and the less we can carry out our God – given mandate and world wide mission. The war in heaven is raging on earth today. Are you being neutralized in the battle?*[7]

A watchman raises a warning voice, Ezekiel gives this warning: *That whosoever heareth the sound of the trumpet, and taketh not warning; if the sword come, and take him away, his blood shall be upon his own head. But if the watchman sees the sword come, and blow not the trumpet, and the people be not warned; if the sword come, and take any person from among them, he is taken away in his iniquity; but his blood will I require at the watchman's hand.*[8]

This earth is nearing a time of cleansing, a time to sweep the floor, and a time to do away with wicked things and wickedness. It will be a time of complete purification and a destruction of evil and evil ways. Signs with warnings on a cosmic scale are all about us, yet, the world, as a whole, is lacking vision ignoring the warnings.

The Lord has said: *And he that taketh not his cross, and followeth after me, is not worthy of me. He that findeth his life shall lose it: and he that loseth his life for my sake shall find it.*[9]

Who's on the Lord's side? President Benson stated: *Never before in our history has there been greater need for faithfulness among our members. Now is the time for all who claim membership in the Church of Jesus Christ of Latter-day Saints to stand firm and demonstrate their allegiance to the Kingdom of God.*[10]

Apostasy and wickedness shall precede the second coming, and the Lord's sword shall fall upon the world.

And also the Lord shall have power over his saints, and shall reign in their midst, and shall come down in judgment upon Idumea, or the world.[11]

For, behold, the Lord will come with fire, and with his chariots like a whirlwind, to render his anger with fury, and his rebuke with flames of fire.[12]

For I know their works and their thoughts: it shall come, that I will gather all nations and tongues; and they shall come, and see my glory.[13]

For by fire and by his sword will the Lord plead with all flesh: and the slain of the Lord shall be many.[14]

For my sword shall be bathed in heaven: behold, it shall come down upon Idumea, and upon the people of my curse, to judgment.[15]

And He shall come in a day of apostasy to destroy the wicked. *And there shall be upon every high mountain, and upon every high hill, rivers and streams of waters in the day of the great slaughter, when the towers fall.*[16]

Therefore I will shake the heavens, and the earth shall remove out of her place, in the wrath of the Lord of hosts, and in the day of his fierce anger.[17]

Howl ye; for the day of the Lord is at hand; it shall come as destruction from the Almighty.[18]

And Babylon, the glory of kingdoms, the beauty of the Chaldees' excellency, shall be as when God overthrew Sodom and Gomorrah.[19]

Their land also is full of silver and gold, neither is there any end of their treasures; their land is also full of horses, neither is there any end of their chariots.[20]

Their land also is full of idols; they worship the work of their own hands, that which their own fingers have made.[21]

For in that day, before the Son of Man shall come, he shall send forth his angels and messengers of heaven.[22]

The harvest is the end of the world, or the destruction of the wicked.[23]

The reapers are the angels, or the messengers sent of heaven.[24]

As, therefore, the tares are gathered and burned in the fire, so shall it be in the end of this world, or the destruction of the wicked.[25]

Break not my commandments for to save your lives; for whosoever will save his life in this world, shall lose it in the world to come.[26]

And now, verily I say these things unto you, that ye may know this, that the coming of the Lord is as a thief in the night.[27]

But the evil servant is he who is not found watching. And if that servant is not found watching, he will say in his heart, My Lord delayeth His coming.[28]

And then his disciples asked him, saying, Master, tell us concerning thy coming?[29]

And he answered them, and said, In the generation in which the times of the Gentiles shall be fulfilled, there shall be signs in the sun, and in the moon, and in the stars; and upon the earth, distress of nations with perplexity, like the sea and waves roaring. The earth also shall be troubled, and the waters of the great deep.[30]

And that servant who knew his Lord's will, and prepared not for his Lord's coming, neither did according to his will, shall be beaten with many stripes.[31]

Then said Jesus unto them, the Law and the prophets testify of me; yea, and all the prophets who have written, even until John, have foretold of these days.[32]

Knowing this first, that in the last days there shall come scoffers, walking after their own lusts.[33]

Denying the Lord Jesus Christ, and saying, Where is the promise of his coming? for since the fathers fell asleep, all things must continue as they are, and have continued as they are from the beginning of the creation.[34]

But the day of the Lord will come as a thief in the night, in the which the heavens shall shake, and the earth also shall tremble, and the mountains shall melt, and pass away with a great noise, and the elements shall be filled with fervent heat; the earth also shall be filled, and the corruptible works which are therein shall be burned up.[35]

NOTES:

1. D&C 1:12-13.
2. Improvement Era, Dec 1962, Elder Benson, 'It Cannot Happen Here', p 910.
3. Improvement Era, Conference Report, Dec 1965, President David O. McKay, p 1073.
4. Conference Report, April 1950, p 159.
5. Improvement Era, Conference Talk, Elder Benson, p 537.
6. Conference Report, April 1952.
7. Improvement Era, Conference Talk, Elder Benson, June 1965, p. 539.
8. Old Testament, Ezekiel 33:4-6.
9. New Testament, St. Matthew 10:38-39.
10. President Benson, "Who's on the Lord's Side? Who?,
    General Conference address, April 1980.
11. D&C 1:36.
12. Old Testament, Isaiah 66:15.
13. Old Testament, Isaiah 66:18.
14. Old Testament, Isaiah 66:16.
15. Old Testament, Isaiah 34:5.
16. Old Testament, Isaiah 30:25.
17. Old Testament, Isaiah 13:13.
18. Old Testament, Isaiah 13:6.
19. Old Testament, Isaiah 13:19.
20. Old Testament, Isaiah 2:7.
21. Old Testament, Isaiah 2:8.
22. JST: Matthew 13:42.
23. JST: Matthew 13:39.
24. JST: Matthew 13:40.
25. JST: Matthew 13:41.
26. JST: Matthew 16:27.
27. JST: Luke 12:44.
28. JST: Luke 12:54.
29. JST: Luke 21:24.
30. JST: Luke 21:25.
31. JST: Luke 12:56.
32. JST: Luke 16:17.
33. JST: 2 Peter 3:3.
34. JST: 2 Peter 3:4.
35. JST: 2 Peter 3:10.

Pull The Drain Plug

Chapter 22

All spirits, whether they are good or evil, are eternal and cannot be destroyed. None were created to be annihilated. Nevertheless we were all in the presence of our Father in Heaven as spiritual children. Satan was one of us. He was a great orator and very persuasive. By his power he was able to influence billions of spirits to follow him in rebellion. Like most dictators he perpetrated an invasion on the rights of God.

Satan lives as a fallen angel. He is a spirit in the form of man created in the image of God, yet he destroys and then abandons: *Thus we see that the devil will not support his children at the last day, but doth speedily drag them down to hell.*[1]

Joseph Smith said: *The punishment of the devil was that he should not have a habitation like men. The devil's retaliation is, he comes into this world, binds up men's bodies, and occupies them himself. When the authorities come along, they eject him from a stolen habitation.*[2]

Satan's rule is totally foreign to the ways of Heaven. It is a form of compulsion. Communism is a form of compulsion as it deprives people of their God given right of agency. Under such doctrine, men turn into puppets, responding to the commands of dictators. The opposite of truth, Satan's avowed purpose is to thwart the plan of God. He will resort to any means, methods or counterfeits to deceive and destroy the children of God.

Today, many among us deny his existence walking around being totally unaware of the dangers lurking around them. We are at war, and the intensity is increasing day by day – hour by hour – minute by minute - year by year. To some, Satan and his armies are fictitious characters created to represent evil - the man with the long pitchfork out looking for victims to cast into Hell. To others, he is just a large serpent.

An ancient prophet Nephi saw our time and declared: *For behold, at that day he shall rage in the hearts of the children of men, and stir them up to anger against that which is good.And others will he pacify, and lull them away into carnal security, that they will say: all is well. . . and thus the devil cheateth their souls, and leadeth them carefully down to hell. And behold, others he flattereth away, and telleth them there is no hell and he saith unto them: I am no devil, for there is none – and thus he whispereth in their ears, until he grasps them with his awful chains, from whence there is no deliverance.*[3]

Satan and his followers were cast down as unembodied spirits to live in the ambient areas of earth. Today they continue their activity of rebellion against God and righteousness. Consequently each spirit denied the experience of being embodied with the elements (clay) in mortality. Because of this they lack God's promise of eternal progress in the subsequent estates of immortality.

Our brother Lucifer, yes our brother, has established *under the earth* a kingdom of evil. Many prophets refer to Lucifer's abode under the earth as a place of "*darkness*",[4] a place "*in the lowest pit, in darkness, in the depths.*"[5]

The prophet Ezekiel speaks about those who die in wickedness after their bodies are placed in *"nether parts of the earth"*, they shall go, *"with them that go down into the pit."*[6] One should be careful not to be found in the devil's territory. Evil ones cannot destroy those who obey the will of the Lord. *"Resist the devil and he will flee from you; draw nigh unto God and he will draw nigh unto you."*[7]

Satan and his followers were cast down to menace God's plan. We are not talking hundreds, thousands or millions, but instead, we are talking billions of evil spirits. We just don't see them with our clay eyes. They, however, see us and know us.

They were cast *under the earth* to exist for the duration of the habitation of the earth by man, in what could be termed "inner darkness". Since their expulsion from Heaven their armies ascend up the mountains and into our habitation – to wage battle from an unseen world. In my opinion, water is their atmosphere just as the air surrounding us is our atmosphere.

A news article titled "Buried Alive" written by Robert S. Boyd made the following comment. "Over half of the earth's life may lie below land, and sea. Biologist is exploring an enormous living world buried below the surface of the earth. Scientists call it the "subsurface biosphere", a dark world where the sun and stars don't shine. Some call it thc Earth's basement."[8]

Let's take a look at the earth beneath our feet. In the center of earth is a super hot inner iron core and surrounding it is a liquid outer core. On top of it is the mantle being a thick layer of hot dense rock and it lies just above the iron core. Where do we live? It's called the crust or earth's rocky shell. This forms the surface. The crust is estimated as little as five miles thick in places.[9]

Nothing on the earth is larger than the Pacific Ocean. It covers approximately one third of the globe and reaches from the Arctic Ocean to the Antarctica and includes twenty-one seas within its borders. It extends more than 11,000 miles and almost halfway around the world. Its deepest point is nearly seven miles below the surface. It has an average depth of 12,925 feet, or close to 2-1/2 miles.[10]

Suppose we could pull a drain plug allowing the Pacific Ocean and other sea waters to drain out leaving no oceans. What would our mortal clay eyes behold? Close your eyes and use your imagination. Picture twenty-five thousand islands or more spread across the Pacific Ocean appearing as tall mountains and at the crust base (ocean floor) extending valleys and rolling hills. Redirecting our eyes upward onto the island of Japan, Philippines and Indonesia what would we see? Their cities, animals and people live on the top of mountains (once islands) extending downward onto beautiful valleys and hills – void of people. Our land mass according to view would increase almost eighty percent (80%). This earth would look entirely different with lands extending in all directions and mostly uninhabited.

NOTES:

1. Book of Mormon, Alma 30:60.
2. D.H.C., Vol V, p. 403.
3. Book of Mormon, 2 Nephi 28:19-22.
4. Old Testament, Psalms 143:3.
5. Old Testament, Psalms 88:6; 28:1; 30:3.
6. Old Testament, Ezekiel 32:18.
7. New Testament, James 4:7-8.
8. Times-News, Twin Falls, Idaho, Sunday March 14, 2010 – Business section, p 7.
9. National Geographic, Our World, p 18.
10. National Geographic, Our World, 1990, p 220.

The World Is A 'Come And Go' Place Chapter 23

Life is like a huge stage with many scenes going on at the same time. We come here as spirits to occupy a physical body and participate in the earthly play. People arrive here daily by the thousands (births) and eventually exit (death) moving on into another sphere. The world is a 'come and go' place.

Where did it all start? It started a long time ago with an ancient set of grandparents – Adam and Eve. The first couple placed upon this planet called earth. We are one extremely large family, billions have come and billions more are yet to come.

Before coming here, God schooled us regarding three distinct levels of this world. The holy scriptures tell us there is *a heaven above,* one *in the earth* and the other *under the earth.* Where are we now, we are *in the earth.* We will be here only a small amount of time compared to our previous life. It's only a short time before we die allowing our spirits to separate returning home.

The Savior said: *And behold, all things have their likeness, and all things are created and made to bear record of me, both things which are temporal, and things which are spiritual; things which are in the heavens above, and things which are on the earth, and things which are in the earth, and things which are under the earth, both above and beneath: all things bear record of me.*[1]

St. John the Apostle said: *And no man in heaven, nor in earth, neither under the earth, was able to open the book, neither to look thereon.*[2]

It is possible the phrase "*in heaven*" refers to a spirit world that surrounds us in a different dimension? It's a world to which a good spirit or angel must pass through a corridor connecting a passageway or tunnel into our world. The phrase "*in earth*" is the mortal world of which we now live, or a physical world requiring a physical body. "*In earth*" we see through clay eyes which are very dim compared to spiritual eyes. A majority of "mortals" do not see visiting spirits all around us. These spirits can be good or evil.

A spirit person arrives here at a precise moment to enter an assigned mortal body. It is not by accident who you are or where you were born. We live we die and move on completing this heavenly cycle. We are God's children.

The phrase "*under the earth*" is a dimension located below us sometimes referred to as Hell. A place I have no desire to live. It is a real world to which Lucifer and his millions of followers dwell. These spirits have access into our sphere or dimension. They can pass through our buildings and visit with ease.

We are now *in the earth* at a very significant time; a time when a great battle is all around us. In a sense, it is the final stages of a great war between good and evil. It is the road of forks with no middle ground. You are either for Christ or Satan.

And there was war in heaven; Michael and his angels fought against the dragon; and the dragon fought and his angels, and prevailed not; neither was their place found any more in heaven. And the great dragon was cast out, that old serpent, called the Devil, and Satan, which deceiveth the whole world: he was cast out into the earth, and his angels were cast out with him.[3]

We are players in this heavenly war. We just don't remember. All of us experienced a loss of memory at the time of our mortal birth. This loss of memory is a test as to whether we choose right or wrong. We are attending an earthly school, and, upon death, our suitcase contains earthly knowledge and deeds. Our eyes are very dim seeing little of warring spirits sometimes surrounding us. Just who are they and from whence did they come?

Listen to the voice of Jesus Christ: *Wherefore, lift up your hearts and rejoice, and gird up your loins, and take upon you my whole armor, that ye may be able to withstand the evil day, having done all, that ye may be able to stand."*[4]

Therefore rejoice ye heavens, and ye that dwell in them. Woe to the inhabiters of the earth and of the sea! for the devil is come down unto you, having great wrath, because he knoweth that he hath but a short time.[5]

Satan is the author of all lies. His mission is to destroy the souls of all men that they might be like him. He has legions of "angels" willing to assist him in carrying out a scheme of destruction. Satan wants dominion over all the earth with those of us whom dwell here. He will stop at nothing to achieve his objectives. Even at this moment he is ensuing an invasion upon our liberty.

Satan's mission is to take possession of our world, to deceive its inhabitants, who have been sent by God the Father to test their integrity. He is a master artist. Joseph Smith stated, *"He has been and still is much underrated."*[6]

Our bodies are created from the elements of planet earth. For this reason we view this beautiful world about us with clay eyes. An angel could be standing next to you unseen. Spirits see one another similar to a mortal person seeing another. It is all quite natural.

William W. Phelps, in 1831, while traveling down the Missouri River in a canoe experienced a daylight vision seeing the "destroyer" riding in power upon the face of the waters.[7] Regarding this incident Joseph Smith received a revelation: *...by the mouth of my servant John, I cursed the waters. Wherefore, the days will come that no flesh shall be safe upon the waters. And it shall be said in days to come that none is able to go up to the land of Zion upon the waters, but he that is upright in heart. I, the Lord, have decreed, and the destroyer rideth upon the face thereof, and I revoke not the decree."*[8]

A waging war encircles this world with an unseen evil war commandeered by Satan and joined in by those mortals who have chosen to follow him. Their common objective is to destroy free agency by putting power into the hands of a few. It is called a New World Order. Beware! It's a time to take a stand for freedom and free agency *or* to cower down by joining ranks of the devil. Let the bells ring on your house top for freedom, justice and liberty. Let the stars and stripes of the United States of America stand forever as a beacon of light.

In the words of the Lord: *Stand, therefore, having your loins girt about with truth, having on the breastplate of righteousness, and your feet shod with the preparation of the gospel of peace, which I have sent mine angels to commit unto you.*[9]

The trump shall sound, *And this shall be the sound of his trump, saying to all people, both in heaven and in earth, and that are under the earth – for every ear shall hear it, and every knee shall bow, and every tongue shall confess, while they hear the sound of the trump, saying: Fear God, and give glory to him who sitteth upon the throne, forever and ever; for the hour of his judgment is come.*[10]

NOTES:

1. Pearl of Great Price, Book of Moses 6:63.
2. New Testament, Revelation 5:3.
3. New Testament, Revelation 12:7-9.
4. D&C 27:15.
5. New Testament, Revelation 12:12.
6. History of the Church, Vol. IV, p 605.
7. D&C 61 – see introduction.
8. D&C 61:14-16, 19.
9. D&C 27:16.
10. D&C 88:104.

Footsteps On The Ceiling

Chapter 24

Several years ago I moved my wife and daughters to Sheridan, Wyoming. At the time houses were hard to find and rent. I made an appointment with a Realtor hoping she could help us find a house which she did, but meeting her was quite interesting.

While speaking with her she stated, "Most of the older houses built before 1900 are haunted. There is a book published and sold in town about the Ghosts of Sheridan." I said, "Wow, that's scary." She goes on, "There is only one house for rent at this time, it was built in the late 1800's, quite fancy, large windows, big wrap around porch with pillars, but very small yard and a super small one-car garage. There are three bedrooms and a family room upstairs, one full bathroom downstairs and a half bathroom upstairs. The laundry room is in the partial basement, and you must walk with your head lowered or you will hit your head." Later while walking in the basement I hit my head.

She then went on to talk about a haunted house book sharing several stories. "Oh, by the way," she said, "I have two ghosts living in my house. Each one has a name and occasionally we talk, I consider them family." I thought, "What a weird lady. I'm glad she's not my neighbor." Before I left I signed the rental agreement and put down a security deposit and first month's rent. We shook hands sealing the agreement. On the way out she commented, "I certainly hope your house isn't one of the houses pictured in that ghost book. Oh, by the way, an old preacher built this house you're renting. He spent a greater part of his life living in that house. He died in his bedroom."

I thought Jolene, Heather and Catrina are going to be very upset with me when they hear my story. But I have no other choice. Rental houses were lacking, and I needed one now. I had to start work in this area and surrounding states immediately.

It's now the first night in our rental house. To get to the bedrooms you must walk up a narrow stairway to the upper level. There is a small family room with three bedrooms, with our bedroom being the middle bedroom. We climbed into bed exhausted, and through the walls the girls are asleep.

We talked quietly about the Realtor and her ghost book hoping our old house is not included in the book. We finally go to sleep. In the middle of night Jolene wakes me up being quite frightened stating she wants to move out immediately because the house is haunted. I told her it wasn't haunted when suddenly there is noise coming from the ceiling just above our heads. *It sounds like footsteps walking across our ceiling* – a lot of footsteps. Things are really going crazy. We had very little sleep, I was ready to get our money back, quit my job and move back to Utah. I did not want to spend another night in a haunted house.

The next day I realized I must solve the ghost problem or we'll soon be on the road again. Getting a tall ladder I make my way to the upper bedroom to investigate. Out of nowhere I see three gray squirrels cruising across a power line crossing the street then onto our roof and into a small circular hole. The squirrels were living in the rafters above our bedroom. No ghosts! The house was a very peaceful place to live and to this day we have fond memories of Sheridan, Wyoming.

A Ride Into Hell

Chapter 25

In the summer of 2003, I had a close call in a Delta 747 Jetliner, making my way from Salt Lake City non-stop to Atlanta, Georgia. I am reading a book, eating a snack, dozing off and on and now approaching the Atlanta International Airport. It is about a five hour flight across country.

The jet pilot comes on the intercom system and says to prepare for turbulent weather. There are thunder heads surrounding the Atlanta area with some rain. Seat belts are now fastened. We're cruising at 15,000 feet. The pilot comes on again stating that we'll be on hold for fifteen minutes because of air traffic. He assures us that we'll be able to make connecting flights on time.

That was the last time we heard from the pilot or co-pilot. I could see lightning flashing below and streaking across a gray sky leaving me with an uneasy feeling something was not right. Our plane is not climbing high enough above these thunder clouds. Suddenly the large 747 takes a drop, its nose pointing downward, almost like its jet engines have stalled leaving us in a free fall. I thought, what's going to happen to me and all these people?

For some reason the back stop on my passenger seat comes unlatched causing it to start flying back and forth. The G-force is such that I cannot lock it into place. Both women and children are screaming, and it seems like an eternity as the plane drops moving closer and closer into a dark gray thunderhead. Lightning is flashing all around us.

One flight attendant is flung against the pilot's door. She grabbed onto anything to prevent her injury. I know I'm going to die. I often wondered if my life would flash before me. No! This wasn't my thought. I thought I certainly hope the impact doesn't hurt too much. I'm fighting to secure my backrest since my seat belt is the only safety device keeping me from flying into the air. It seems like an eternity. All of a sudden the drop stops, our pilot is now able to pull the plane on course. We circle several times and approach a landing field. No more screaming, all the people are quiet no comments one to another. You could hear a pin drop. It was very, very quiet.

There is no exchange of communication or comment from the pilot. The 747 lands, and we prepare to exit. No one is speaking. You can still hear a pin drop. The exit doors are opened with stairs pointing down. Still no pilots to greet you on your exit. I'm dumbfounded as to the absence of the pilot and co-pilot.

Yes, it was a drop; I thanked God for being alive along with all the other passengers.

How about a ride into a world under the earth's surface some call Hell. I have experienced four types of dreams: heaven dreams, normal, others all jumbled up and several from the evil one. What is the difference between a dream and an out of body experience? When having an out of body experience, you travel quickly. You are among others or just viewing into a different sphere.

What about angels? There are two types good and evil. Can the devil give you visions? Yes he can. For what purpose? You may be on his list.

Being on his list, I have experienced a ride into hell. It was very real and I felt ten times the fear I felt with the unlatched back seat with only a seat belt in the 747 to Atlanta. The free fall of the 747 is incomparable to what I'm about to share with you.

I dreamt I found myself at a factory of some sort in a different world visiting with the employees. It is a large spacious factory with many rooms. Many faceless people worked making trinkets out of metal.

The workers labor at a very slow pace lacking in motivation. As I walk about observing their work, they seem to nod their heads in my direction. This factory has different levels with many stairs going from one level to another. The rooms are dismal in color yet an attempt is made by each spirit of being cordial to my visit.

The factory has gloomy shades of gray, like a cloud covered day with little sunlight. No one has the light of Christ within them; their spirits are lacking even though it is a spirit without a body. For some reason their thoughts are not allowed to come upon me.

My tour guide is a lady who leads me out onto a platform with other people lined up entering a type of indescribable vehicle designed for travel. We're all standing and soon will be holding on for dear life.

Instantly our vehicle drops toward the center of the earth at an unbelievable speed with G-forces upon me uncomparable to a roller coaster or even the 747 Jet Plane drop. It was very real, and I was in fear for my life, my family, my friends and others who may at sometime end up onto this ride.

The intensity of speed increases, now many are screaming "God Save Me", "Oh God Please Save Me" and fear intensified even more upon my soul. It was very dark no light it was like being in a cave pointing downward or a runaway elevator with the lights turned out. Soon I cried out, "Oh, God Save Me." As soon as the words left my mouth the falling vehicle suddenly stopped.

I was now in a new world underneath our earth. Our vehicle soon disappeared with each left standing. It was a world enclosed with a high glass wall surrounding its open areas.

On the other side was a large building of brick similar to a city building with many windows. Beyond its left side was an area of many acres. A fair was taking place with riders, booths, and people walking about participating in whatever was going on. It seemed very inferior to county fairs in the world above me.

The people about me walked through the glass wall making their way amongst others visiting different rides and booths. I had no desire to join in or walk with them. My only thought was to telephone Jolene. I felt alone being very far away into the depths of hell with no transportation to make a trip back up into our world. Written on the glass before me was a phone number. I thought, I need my cell phone and by dialing this number I can talk with Jolene telling her of my whereabouts. Then it occurred to me I don't know my whereabouts. This unusual experience soon ended.

Shaking In My Shoes

Chapter 26

All around the world are evil spirits wandering, waiting for an opportunity to tempt us or by sending an evil thought within our minds. These spirits have the means and technology to affect our dreams, pass through our houses and look over our shoulders. If allowed they can pass through or stay within our bodies.

In 1974 President Harold B. Lee shared an encounter with an evil spirit. *I want to bear you my solemn witness that I know there are [evil] forces in the world today. It would seem to me somewhat significant – as I have thought about it, that the first and only experience of its kind I have ever had, came shortly after I came into the Council of the Twelve when I was asked to administer to a young woman who was possessed of an evil spirit. Seemingly, there might have been a purpose in letting me know that these powers were around.*[1]

One year we attended the Snake River Festival. I noticed a young man and two girls of high school age heading toward the river. One of the teenage boys wore a t-shirt that said in large print "I AM EVIL" and he wore a ball cap with a Hitler swastika. It occurred to me that this young man can attend high school and nothing would be said as to the message on his shirt and hat. Yet if he wore a t-shirt stating 'I LOVE JESUS' the high school would expel him from school. It's the law of the land.

What has happened to this 'nation under God'? If you take a Bible in your lunch box to the public schools, you'll be expelled. Bow your head and say a blessing verbally on your lunch, and you'll be expelled. However, if you do an obscene jester or use foul language it will be overlooked. I've always had the opinion that what you think is eventually what you'll become. There is no middle road you must choose either evil or good. It's very evident that this young man chose evil.

I'm the type of person who can feel evil spirits and know of their presence. It is a gift, and one I experienced in the mission field. My first real experience was while doing my laundry at a Laundromat in Opa Locka, Florida. My missionary companion Elder Douglas Stroup watched his dirty clothes tumble in the machine as I went to get change from the attendant. I pulled a $10 bill from my pocket and gave it to the attendant for change. As he walked away I was left standing counting my money. To my astonishment I counted eleven dollars. I wondered why he made this mistake.

The dim room was in the main foyer of the Laundromat. I was left standing by myself. Before I had time to think I looked up spotting a dark figure in the shape of a man flying through the air toward me. This figure passed into my body and a voice said, "Keep it." Shaking in my shoes, I commanded it in the name of Jesus Christ to leave which it did. I viewed it as it passed out of my body going through a wall of the darkened room. I then found the attendant, explained his error in money change returning the dollar. This evil experience really shook me up. It is just as vivid today as it was 46 years ago.

Suppose I had kept the extra dollar? I think there would have been an extra companion following me on my mission. This companion, although unseen, would have destroyed my efforts as a missionary and passed other temptations into my path.

I spent fourteen years as a vocational instructor of auto mechanics, drafting, and welding on a high school level. I'm very familiar with the progressive movement regarding the National Education Association (NEA). During those years, we as teachers, looked upon the Parent-Teacher-Association (PTA), our local School Board and the State Education Association as our directive representing the people. Somehow along the way it has reversed direction allowing the U.S. President extending an arm of authority NOT THE PEOPLE.

Parents, do you know what your children are being taught in school? Teachers are no longer allowed to use the words 'man', 'woman', 'mom and dad'. The words 'policeman', 'fireman', 'mailman', 'shop foreman', etc. are now eliminated. The proper tone is 'parents', 'firepersons', 'mailperson' and so on. It is called using the proper gender and it requires teacher certification.

In 1969 a warning was given by an apostle of the Lord, Elder Ezra Taft Benson: *Today we face insidious, devastating evils that are wide spread. Aimed especially at the destruction of America – the last great bastion of freedom – with emphasis on our youth, the evils are everywhere, sponsored, promoted, and directed by the Communist conspiracy, fellow travelers, and dupes. Never has evil been presented in such an array of appealing forms. We face a most dangerous revolution in America and it is now in progress.*[2]

The godless Communists have declared, "We are going to destroy the moral character of a generation of young Americans, and when we have finished you will have nothing with which to really defend yourself against us." We may, as adults, close our eyes to them and keep our heads in the sand, hoping they will go away; but these evils are here, close by, working insidiously and destructively day by day, hour by hour, without ceasing. Will parents who have abandoned their responsibilities for the training and guidance of their children awaken and act before it is too late?[3]

These atrocious, destructive evils are now revealed in our music, in our art, in sex perversion and so-called sex education in the schools, in destructive sensitivity training – a powerful form of Pavlovian brainwashing, as used by Communists on captured American servicemen in Korea and by Hitler in Nazi Germany.

These evils are prominent in the promotion of drugs – LSD, marijuana, and a host of others – in leading magazines and underground publications for youth; in TV, movie, and radio programs, in pornographic literature, in morally destructive paperback books available to all on newsstands, and in Communist-oriented anti-American organizations, such as SDS (Students for a Democratic Society).

These devilish forces "led generally by dirty minds in dirty bodies" seem to be everywhere. They are spreading into every segment of our social, economic, and religious life – all aimed at the destruction of one whole generation of our choice youth in preparation for the Communist take-over.[4]

These words of warnings were addressed to us 41 years ago at the 139th Semiannual General Conference of the Church. How much further along have we traveled at this time?

Elder Benson continues: *Some of the most prominent targets now under withering fire in this war against us are the Ten Commandments, the Sermon on the Mount, the Constitution of the United States, the institution of private property, and the basic concepts of the gospel of Jesus Christ.*

Surely this is a time when consideration might well be given by the people of America, and the entire free world, to the important matter of citizenship responsibility and more importantly, membership in the churches of the free world.

Put on the whole armour of God, that ye may be able to stand against the wiles of the devil. For we wrestle not against flesh and blood, but against principalities, against powers, against the rulers of the darkness of this world, against spiritual wickedness in high places."[5]

If we listen to evil and 'keep the extra dollar' our freedoms will soon become a dream and overnight our world will be different. Our Pledge of Allegiance will be to 'Mother Earth' and not to our God who looks upon us.

NOTES:

1. Ensign Magazine, February 1974, p 16.
2. The Improvement Era, Dec 1969, Godless Forces Threaten Us, by Elder Ezra Taft Benson, p 29.
3. Ibid, p 70.
4. Ibid.
5. Holy Bible, Eph. 6:11-12.

Time To Move On Chapter 27

There is a place where we in our pre-mortal life prepared ourselves for life on earth. Each of us were very desirous of coming here to what we now call mortal life. We came here as mature spirits. We looked upon this life as an opportunity to learn many things and develop the attributes to which we lack.

We came here with different personalities, talents, intelligences, and of different ages depending upon our spiritual birth in our pre-life. A veil of forgetfulness is placed over each of us as we enter into our new bodies. We no longer remember our pre-mortal life and from whence we came. Mortal life is a testing ground to see whether we choose good or evil; it is a chance to use our free agency.

Some grow up into maturity and on into what we call the golden age. Others may separate (or die) as a baby, child, teenager, young adult or as an adult. It all depends upon the circumstances, our genetics, or sometimes the course we choose to follow in our lives.

Separation is a term used to which our spirit leaves our mortal body and returns to God. We refer to this as death. The earth body is left behind by our spirit. The spirit is eternal and moves on into the world above us.

What we accumulate here in worldly goods stays here. We return there as we came - a mature spirit without a suitcase. However, knowledge, experiences (whether good or evil), habits acquired, deeds unto others, personality and accomplishments, newly acquired talents, etc. is the only luggage we take with us.

Our spirit can slip away from our body very quickly depending upon the circumstances to which death occurs. Some deaths are traumatic. The spirit and body may separate before experiencing much pain such as in a fire, a severe car accident or torture in prison.

You suddenly die what are your choices? You still have your free agency. You may want to hang around for a little bit. Nevertheless, there will be someone (relative or friend) to greet you, so be patient if they are running a little bit late. It may be a moment or two for you to actually realize you're dead. The realization hits you that you can actually float and walk through walls. People don't see you. You can look over their shoulder, and they don't notice you. However, they may feel your spirit.

We are given the choice to remain *in* this *earth* until our bodies are buried or move onto the heaven from whence we came. More than likely, most of us will choose to remain for a short time to comfort our loved ones before we move on.

Some may linger around for a time. There are some who die as atheists, some bonded by bodily appetites or other earthly commitments, may find it hard to move on. Some can't follow the light pulling them toward God. They need to let go of this world by moving toward the light.

We are all God's children. He loves each of us. We each stood up and voted for free agency. That free agency is still within us even unto death and into the next world.

How do we get the light of Christ in our lives? By doing what is right and controlling our thoughts. All of us come into this life with the light of Christ in us regardless of race, creed or color. We're all brothers and sisters and children of God.

Yes, we are here for an earthly education. We came here willing to make sacrifice for each other - some call it charity - looking after your neighbor before self. Everything is done for the growth of our spirits. Each of us has talents not be hidden.

The most important thing to do in this life is to think of others before self. Our Savior always thought of others before himself. Being the Creator he set the example for all of us. What is so hard in this life? Just to take time out and think of others before self and then go into action and do it. But to love others you really need to love yourself.

Strange Happenings Chapter 28

Writing and publishing the book 'Keeper of the Prophet's Sword' in 2009 was not an easy task. It required a lot of time, faith, prayers and guidance. Many times I felt the Holy Ghost prompting me in my research. It was really a test between good and evil. It was almost like our yard, garden area and home was a battle front. Attempts were made to injure me anytime the Prophet's sword was kept in our house.

My first awareness was an arrow darting at me. It was a life or death situation. On an early afternoon I was returning home from Utah with the sword on the back seat of my truck. It was covered with an Indian blanket. Eighteen miles from home I decided to take a short cut exiting off I-84 onto the Malta highway. It ended up being a bad decision. It is a two-lane highway lacking a painted center line. This country road is lined with sagebrush and an occasional cottontail, jack rabbit or deer scurrying across the road. At times trucks hauling cattle, hay, grain, corn or sugar beets occupy it.

I'm relaxed listening to country music on the radio and enjoying the weather. Little did I know my life and the prophets' sword soon would be in jeopardy. Driving slightly above the speed limit, I approach a double trailer semi-truck, so I lighten up on the gas pedal creating a distance between me and the truck. I turned off the radio making no rash decision to pass the truck.

Suddenly another truck driving in the opposite direction and passing the semi-truck I am following pulls into my lane pointing directly at me. It's shooting like an arrow toward my vehicle. It's decision time. The two-lane highway's shoulder dips into a barrow pit or slops into a fence line. It left me with only three choices; one, hit the truck head on; two, brake down staying in my lane and pray the driver of the truck will wake up and at the last minute pull into his lane. Perhaps I could pull over into his lane as he darts past me hoping that he stays in my lane as we pass each other. And three, drive my truck into the barrow pit at the last second which would surely cause a rollover and several flips. It is a very scary situation with just a second or two in determining my fate and those of the relics.

I thought "Hang on it's now time to ditch the truck. Will it hurt? I don't know." Just at this moment I'm staring into the face of the other driver. He almost looked like he was in a trance of some sort. He suddenly pulls back into his lane. Wow! That was a close call.

So far there are two events to ponder upon - the lightning strike six months earlier with my granddaughter Kassidy and now this. What's next? Only three months until the publication of my book *Keeper of the Prophet's Sword.*

Surprise! Two weeks later another strange event occurs. I'm working on my book around 9:00 a.m., our dogs Sage and Smokey are acting very peculiar running around but not barking. What now?

The door bell rings several times in sequence like an alarm going off. I answer the door. Standing before me is a farmer looking very excited and big eyed. He states, "I can't believe it. I just can't believe it. It's my lucky day. I need to go buy some lottery tickets. It must be my lucky day". I stand in amazement asking what is going on. He points to the north side of my house as we walk off the porch. Wow, it's my lucky day too.

He was driving his large tractor down the road at 30 mph towing a two-ton grain cultivator which came unhitched making its way toward the center of our house.

At the time, I was sitting in our music room reading a book not realizing a piece of machinery was unhitched and aimed directly in my path. Angels were here. Why else would the machinery take a 180° turn to the north passing the large pine tree and stopping about a foot from the corner of our house? Yes, it was a lucky day for the farmer.

The next event is two weeks later. A beautiful crab apple tree takes center stage in our front yard. It is surrounded with a blanket of Kentucky bluegrass circling its base and lower trunk. It stands tall with extruding branches giving the appearance of being a protector with an armor of frost. It seems to whisper out "What will I do today if I am brave?"

The base of the tree measures forty-five inches in circumference. It is a hardwood, very dense and strong with no bend. The age is approximately fifty years if you counted the rings.

In the late fall, I pruned off several large branches to enhance the beauty of the tree. Later this proved to be a very wise decision, especially for one particular branch on the lower end facing to the north. The tree displays two personalities. It produces two sets of blossoms: one flower of dark pink with a dark green leaf and another with a light pink flower. May through June it is a massive bloom and one to behold.

The crab apple tree is not alone. It has a friend just a few feet away. It is a large Blue Spruce Pine spanning a large base, thick and very tall. The tree borders our neighbor's side yard. Birds by the hundreds frequent these trees. Many varieties join together as a singing chorus into the upper branches. The smaller birds seem to like the old crab apple tree with its many pink flowers and blossoms.

In our house at that time was the sword of the Prophet Joseph Smith. In the next few weeks my book, *Keeper of the Prophet's Sword,* will be ready for publication. Anytime the relics are in our home we can feel the spirit and protection. Nevertheless it seems like a battle is going on between good and evil. Very strange things are happening all around us, sometimes I fear for my life. As mentioned a truck on the Malta highway moved into my lane directly at me; the lightning strike on the backside of the fence; a wandering farm machine coming off the street heading toward the center of our house; and several evil encounters. What's next?

Daylight is on the rise when suddenly, out of nowhere, comes a very *loud thump* shaking our house almost like an earthquake. My first thought is "Oh no, it's happening again." It's seems like the movie Groundhog Day, starring Bill Murray (which is one of my favorite movies).

A tan Nissan came off the street directly toward my truck just below our bedroom. The car hit the crap apple tree dead center with a very loud thud causing damage by throwing the windshield forward into pieces extruding some twenty-five feet forward toward the driveway also impacting glass into the tree. The large tree did not budge, only some bark damage and a center crack. Somehow the car was still able to operate with the driver immediately backing up off the lawn onto the road. The driver somehow managed to drive away clunking down the street.

For the life of me, I don't know how the driver was able to drive his vehicle away so suddenly. Surely the glass showered his face. It would be like hitting a cement block. The tree branch I pruned off had saved his life; it would have been a direct hit into his face.

I hurried down the bedroom stairs and out the front door to inspect the damage. I was greatly amazed as I glanced at the entry angle onto the lawn. The early morning sun was up the highway was dry and there was no explainable reason for the automobile to veer off the road.

I inspect the highway entry comparing the tire marks to the farmer's unhitched grain machinery. I can't believe my eyes. Both the farm machinery and auto tracks were only inches away from each other as they shot like arrows toward the house. It was a miracle. How could this be and what are the odds? One in a billion – I don't know. However I do know both incidents were directed toward me and the prophet's sword.

Suppose the tree wasn't there? It had a direct line towards our bedroom. If the car had been able to continue, it would have hit my truck and into the garage more than likely taking out the support beam supporting the upstairs bedroom. The crab apple tree saved our house and possibly our lives.

Two weeks later a strange fog circles the house. It's around 3 a.m., and I'm observing the weather noticing that it is very strange. As I look out the bedroom window a howling wind is blowing a ground level white drifting cloud across our yard. The yard light lightens the flowing cloud leaving an eerie feeling upon me. There is no darkness; the light seems to filter into a rapidly moving cloud. Jolene is awakened and taking in the strange event. Visiting birds are clinging on for dear life amongst the branches of the large pine trees.

We are in wonderment as to the power of flying clouds when out of nowhere a loud *bang* and flash of light from the back yard. It lightens up our bedroom and the voice of thunder shakes the house. A lightning bolt struck the yard light pole causing the lights to flicker off-on-off and then stays on. What in the world is going on these are just low level clouds floating across the yard.

The fireworks are in the making and suddenly aloud thundering *bang* shakes the front of the house as a bolt of lightning strikes a pole transformer. Dairy lights to the east as well as the surrounding area go off extending into three hours. Jolene immediately calls the electric company to report the incident letting them know of a lightning strike upon the transformer. The winds with low level white clouds soon pass, and it's almost time for church.

After church we walk the back yard sadly viewing dead birds scattered near the fence lines. The light pole shows no damage however the front yard transformer does show heat damage on one side.

Monday morning Jolene called the power company to inquire regarding the transformer to see if any other lightning strikes hit the area. A representative stated that a substation went down for several hours. There were no lightning strikes reported in the area. A technician later stopped by noting an indication of heat damage to our transformer. Nevertheless, the power grid meter on the pole did not show any surge.

Again two weeks later another incident strikes the yard. On an early Sunday morning just south of our house we hear a "*Bang, Bang, Bang, Bang, and Bang.*"

A Chevrolet Suburban took out the south fence splintering five railroad ties into pieces. It is quite evident our house and yard is a war zone anytime the Prophet's sword is nearby. Flying arrows seem to come out of nowhere. Truthfully it is very strange not knowing future events or what to expect. It seems never ending.

At times I ask myself what is going on. It's a book, it's a sword, it's an oak casket stick, yet, I sense a real threat is upon me. Just the other day a friend, Dennis Crane, stopped by making a friendly comment, "Howard, your place is almost like you're living in the Bermuda Triangle with all these strange happenings." Dennis, as a neighbor, has viewed many of the happenings. If you don't believe it, just ask him. As you read further into this book, you will see that it is only the beginning.

At that time I almost wanted to stop writing my book, truly retire, hit the fishing hole on the Snake River, taking it easy and doing whatever made me happy. But that would have been just a temporary fix and would soon pass.

Man is on the earth to be tested. The issue as to whether he succeeds or fails will be determined by how he uses his agency. His whole future, through all eternity, is at stake. Abridge man's agency, and the whole purpose of his mortality is thwarted.

No, I did not quit writing the book and it is now selling across the world.

Eyes With No Light

Chapter 29

The Mormon pioneers brought into the Salt Lake Valley three great volumes of new scripture to which gave a great deal of new information regarding the past and future of America the Land of Promise. These scriptures make it clear that God's hand has been instrumental to the establishment of this nation.

Just think what this world would be like if there had never been a United States of America. It would be far different, a more unhappy place. Communism and socialism would rule. At this time, our nation is in serious trouble opposed by Satan himself with many who chose to follow after him.

Just who are we fighting and how large in scope is this war? It is much larger in scope than we as mortals with clay eyes realize.

One Sunday morning Jolene and I were watching Devotionals on BYU TV, and the speaker was lecturing on keeping our families safe from evil. He spoke of a dream his Stake President had and the relevance it was to keeping the family safe. I will try and relay it to you to the best of my ability. This man (Stake President) dreamed he was in his back yard with his family – wife, children and grandchildren – enjoying one another's company when he noticed a large flock of birds flying into the neighborhood. As they got closer to his house he noticed they were black birds that were pairing off into groups of two and flying into each yard in the subdivision. He noticed the birds would fly into an open window or door of each house. As he pondered about the birds he became concerned for his family ushering them into the house for safety. He realized these birds represented evil, the birds were there to bring evil into the house and turn the inhabitants away from Jesus Christ. He glanced around making sure all his family was there. He was certain all the doors and windows were locked tightly so the birds could not get into his house. As his dream progressed he realized that one window downstairs was open ever so slightly and two birds were in his house. He woke up with a start from the dream realizing that he still had work to do in his own family to keep evil out of their lives and keep his family safe.

Three days before the publication of my book, *Keeper of the Prophet's Sword,* I had an unusual dream.

I found myself standing midpoint in a four way intersection. It is a large unusual city and my view was unlimited in all directions. It occurred to me this is downtown. Crowds of well dressed people both men and women with bags in their hands were making their way along and in and out of buildings. The men had no ties or jackets. The women wore causal wear. I was under the earth's surface in a strange city.

All the buildings looked the same; two story side by side lacking personality. They were of the same color that being desert sand. All the roofs were flat. I could view thousands of people mingling and shopping.

The sky was very unusual with no sun or clouds. It was more like a gray blue color, yet the light was abundant. No power poles. There were no children; just a lot of adults. There was a wide walkway with a pavement of red orange color bricks.

Wanting to view their faces, I hurriedly walked from the intersection and joined the crowd. I was able to move among them unnoticed. Looking upon their faces I was awe struck for they lacked the spirit of Christ in their eyes. It became very obvious this was an underworld of people living under the direction of Satan.

The following night, I found myself standing in the exact location of the intersection that I stood in the previous dream. It was the same time of day and seemed to be in the same circumstances however the streets are void of people. This time I noticed a large man walking toward me. When he is almost upon me, I looked up at him. He is nearly seven feet tall and well dressed. From a man's point of view he is good looking. He is wearing a dark sport jacket, gray shirt, black pants and fancy shoes. He appears to be approximately 40 years of age as to our world and had neatly trimmed thick black hair. His image is burned into my memory. I thought could this possibly be Satan? I don't know. The only thing I do know is he is well built and walks with authority.

In his left hand is my book *Keeper of the Prophet's Sword* and he speaks to me with authority as he raises my book into the air above his head. He says, "Howard, this book is no good, and it has to stop now. Did you hear me? It has to stop now." I'm shaking in my shoes, and instantly he threw my book upon the brick intersection where it was shredded into pieces.

Looking away from him I notice a man standing near me who is short in stature – about five feet tall. He is dressed in causal wear and is quite bald with just a little hair above his ears. His image is also burned into my memory. As he looks up at me I am able to view into his eyes. He has the eyes of an evil demon.

It's now time for the first printing of my new book. I'm advised by Bill Nichols, the owner of Blip Color, to be there no later than 8 a.m. stating: "It will only take one hour to print and bind 1,500 books." It's my first book and I'm so excited that I can't wait to be on my way. While driving to Blip Color I think of the tall man shredding my book. Hopefully it won't happen but it seemed so real.

Guess what happened? We had to shred the first three hundred books off the press. A black mark smeared across the face of Joseph Bates Noble's picture in the front section and a black smear went across my picture in the back section. This event had never happened before on Bill's printing press. Bill and his crew spent nine hours printing the first 1,500 books. I was there the entire day. I guess the 'tall man' did follow up with his threat.

The book *Keeper of the Prophet's Sword* turned out beautifully. Printed in color on quality paper many people in my travels have commented as to the workmanship of Blip Color.

A Flying Truck

Chapter 30

Using your imagination, picture in your mind a huge cannon stationed on an overpass spanning a six lane freeway (I-15) near Ogden, Utah. Three lanes point south, three lanes point north, and are separated by a cement barrier. It is Thursday, 9:30 a.m. The cannon is primed, loaded and ready to fire. The intended victim is the author of this book.

Slipping back into time, at age 18 I joined the Utah Army National Guard. My MOS was Howitzer guns. After boot camp, my assigned base was "Fort Sill" near Lawton, Oklahoma. My rank was an E-5 or sergeant. Wow, that was fifty years ago. It seems like yesterday. My responsibility was number one gunner. I cut the powder strings, loaded the charge and helped in placing the shell projectile into the cannon barrel and close the breach block. Our targets consisted of old junk cars placed in an open field just west of Lawton. The big gun (cannon) was a one-five-five Howitzer.[1]

155 mm Howitzer M-114 at the U.S. Army Field Artillery Museum, Ft. Sill, Oklahoma

Rate of fire burst: 4 rounds per minute

Sustained: 40 rounds per hour

Muzzle velocity 563 m/s (1,847 ft/s)

Maximum range 14,600m (15,967 yds)

Surveyors coordinated adjustments for the target. The big Howitzer Cannons were adjusted vertically up or down, to the left or to the right to be zeroed in on the junk car. So basically, we followed the directions of the surveyors and our commander. The first shot is getting the coordination. The second shot usually is a dead ringer – or right on target.

One time a shell blew up a vacant house in a new subdivision. This did not go well with the town people. The officer in charge was quickly reduced in rank and shipped off to another army base.

Fast forward to today and I make my way one early morning to Utah in my small Toyota Corolla. It is loaded with my books as well as a few emergency items. These included a flashlight, candle stick, extra coat, warm gloves, pullover orange stocking cap, snow boots, first aid kit, several candy bars and bottled water. A suitcase is included with extra clothes just in case the trip required an overnight stay. I like to be prepared. It's easier on the mind, more relaxing and the drive more enjoyable. I had an uneasy feeling about traveling between Snowville and Tremonton, Utah, so I took an hour snooze at the gas station in Snowville. The fog was thick enough that it would require a double edged sword to cut through it.

When I awake the sun is on the rise, the fog is lifting and it was time to meet my schedule. I had bookstores to call on from Ogden to Salt Lake City, a four o'clock appointment in Bountiful with Sandy J. Inman and Commissioner Tom Tolman. Our topic will center on a July fundraiser for a new Bountiful Historical Museum.

This is to be a kick-off event with other events to follow throughout the year. Friday will be a day to celebrate the United States Constitution. Saturday is an LDS focus day displaying Joseph Smith's sword as well as speakers touching on several topics. It's a big event for the sword as it was hidden away for 160 years in West Bountiful by Joseph Bates Noble and his family.

Around 9:15 a.m. I am driving south in the early morning traffic into Ogden. I become quite apprehensive so I turn off the radio and turn my attention to the traffic flow. I am cruising at 70 mph in a 65 mph zone of the I-15 freeway. A lot of traffic is on either side of my Corolla and the rear view mirror reflects a two trailer semi-truck at my rear.

I come upon the Riverdale Road overpass when my mind reverts back to my National Guard days. Suddenly, the stationary cannon has fired. The target is me. I wonder who pulled the trigger? I have three seconds before I'm dead. Twenty-eight feet above me out of nowhere a white, three-quarter-ton, Chevrolet truck flies off the overpass, shoots up an additional ten feet falling directly toward my windshield. It's almost like being in a three dimensional movie with the glasses on.

According to the Utah Highway Patrol, the truck slid onto the top barrier of the Riverdale overpass flying off into the air. The driver drives at a high speed and had also been drinking. It was almost like going duck hunting, shooting a Mallard high in the sky, watching it fall downward at a high speed directly into your face. The reaction time at most would be three seconds. I felt like a spider on the kitchen floor waiting to be smashed under foot. It's over – it's over – I'm dead! God please save me!

Suddenly an angel was on my right side. I felt his power and presence. His hands were on my hands. A foot was upon the brake pedal. Instantly the car dropped in speed and somehow the steering wheel turned slightly to the right pulling the car from the center lane of traffic to the right lane. Oh, my gosh! There is no time to check my side or rear view mirrors. I'm dead either way. Move to the right, and I'm crushed by a semi-truck move to the left, and I'm dead with the flying truck. What do I do? The angel took charge, and saved my life. I'm greatly indebted to him and sincerely thank him from the bottom of my heart. The angel reacted like the speed of light. It's hard to share or explain unless you were there in my shoes.

Rushing downward the upside down truck hits the pavement with a crushing blow like a stick of dynamite. It exploded with a sound of thunder. The plastic, headlights, tool box, spare tire and other parts of the truck are flying in front of me. The truck hits just to the left front of my car, narrowly missing my bumper. It seems as though my Corolla flies over the glass, headlights, spare tire, tool box and other items flying onto the lane. Surprisingly there are no scratches or damage to my car. It's a miracle.

Upon impact the truck bounces into the air approximately fifteen feet then turns upright landing onto the cement barrier separating the south and north bound traffic. My thoughts were the occupant could not be alive, he's dead.

Immediately I check my mirrors; I'm completely in awe. No traffic to either side or behind me. It's a miracle. How can this be? The early morning traffic in Ogden on I-15 is always bumper to bumper. I'm alive! Thank you God and please bless the occupant of the flying truck.

I'm shaking like a leaf in the wind; making my way under the bridge spanning I-15 and stopping a few hundred yards off to the right side of the pavement. Somehow I manage to dial 911 on my cell phone, holding my finger to hit the numbers. I report the accident. Others are calling in at the same time.

I must get out quickly and help the victim. Looking behind there are at least 15 people rushing across the freeway to assist. There is much more to this story; nevertheless, I'm bringing it to a close as it is hard to share my feelings.

Quoting a member of the Quorum of the Twelve Apostles, Elder Jeffrey R. Holland: *From the beginning down through the dispensations, God has used angels as His emissaries in conveying love and concern for His children."*

Usually such beings are not seen. Sometimes they are. But seen or unseen they are always near. Sometimes their assignments are very grand and have significance for the whole world. Sometimes the messages are more private. Occasionally the angelic purpose is to warn.[2]

Article in Deseret News

Ogden man dies a week after crash.

Published: Wednesday, February 3, 2010 5:09 p.m. MST

Ogden – A Ogden man has died from the injuries he suffered after his pickup truck fell 28 feet onto I-15 last month, landing on its hood. John (last name withheld by author), 48, died Monday at McKay-Dee Hospital, said Utah Highway Patrol Sgt. Jimmy Higgs. John never regained consciousness following the January 14 crash, Higgs said.

Troopers say he was going from southbound I-15 to eastbound I-84 when he lost control of his pickup, which hit a concrete barrier and slid along it for a short time before falling over and dropping onto I-15 below. The truck then bounced from its hood onto its tires.

Higgs said alcohol use was believed to have been a factor in the crash; however, no charges were pursued against him because of his medical condition.

Geoff Liesik[3]

NOTES:

1. M114 – 155mm Howitzer, online from Wikipedia, the free encyclopedia.
2. The Ministry of Angels, by Jeffry R. Holland, Ensign.
3. Deseret News, Ogden man dies a week after crash, By Geoff Liesik, Published Wednesday, February 3, 2010. To see the accident- refer to Standard Examiner, Friday, January 15, 2010 www.standard.net

A Black Bird Upon a Mailbox

Chapter 31

As I start my early morning walk the light of day is upon me. The air is brisk and my .38 revolver is tucked away in my pants pocket. In my black jacket pocket is a bottle of water. A camouflage stocking cap covers my head It will be a great day.

What can go wrong? It's just me walking along a farmer's dirt road. A ring neck pheasant jumps suddenly from a ditch bank darting over my head into the early morning sky. It is highly unusual to see a pheasant these days. I marvel at the beauty surrounding me; snow capped mountains, the Snake River hidden away in the low lands, plowed fields in all directions with newly arrived birds lining the power lines.

Sometimes along my walk I spot a gaggle of geese, a stray dog, a jack rabbit, a mallard duck hidden away in the ditch bank, or a coyote streaking across the farmer's field. I also like to look for small unusual rocks along the base of the road. At times my pockets are lined with rocks.

The brisk air clears my mind. It's been several weeks since the flying truck incident in Ogden Utah. The closeness of death still dwells in my thoughts. Today I extend my walk eventually reaching the midway point. I take a break and a sip of my water.

An uneasiness comes upon me, and the tranquility of my morning walk is no longer. I decide to go a different direction. In my view is a house several hundred yards across the field. Suddenly a man comes out of his back door firing a large caliber pistol at a can on a post. The shots ring loud with steel bullets raining around me. One bullet whistles through the air nearly clipping off my left ear. I could feel the rush of air darting on all sides. I drop to the ground face first. Why is he firing at me? Mud is on my face and into my teeth. It brought back memories of army boot camp dodging bullets and dropping to the ground.

The showering of lead subsided. After getting my composure I stand up wiping the mud from my jacket then headed over to his house. When he answered the door I explained the situation of the flying bullets. He was greatly embarrassed and apologetic.

Jokingly I asked him, "Why are you shooting at me?" His mouth dropped open stating, "I'm sorry your black clothing faded into the background." This man is a really good person. He was just practice shooting at a tin can on top a post. I just happened to be at the wrong spot at the right time. It reminds me of Samuel the Lamanite standing upon the wall speaking to the Nephites with a showering of arrows.

Standing on the grass we shared experiences. I mentioned my .38 pistol and my concealed carry license. Jokingly he asked me, "Why didn't you fire back at me?" Smiling I said, "You're my friend, I would never think of doing such a thing. But thinking back on it maybe I should have fired into the air as a distress call." He smiled.

Across the road sits his mailbox. A black bird is standing on top staring in our direction. It seemed unusual as birds usually fly away when hearing loud gun shots, especially when a series of shots are fired. Staring at the black bird he suggests that I shoot it off the mailbox. Jokingly I told him that I couldn't do this I might put a hole through it. He stated: "It's just an old mailbox and it wouldn't hurt anything." I told him I couldn't fire a bullet at the black bird. He understood, we shook hands, and I continued my walk.

Return Of The Body Guards

Chapter 32

Shortly after all these strange events (the shredding of my book, flying truck and dodging of bullets) I was invited to speak and share the sacred relics at a fireside to be held at the West Bountiful First Ward. This was very special to me because I had attended this Ward as a youth and I gave my 'missionary homecoming' address there.

The original chapel was built in early 1876-1877. My great-grandfather William Reed Smith was the Stake President during that time, and Joseph Bates Noble served as Bishop of this Ward for a number of years.

The chapel was torn down about the same time Joseph Bates Noble's adobe house was torn down. The new chapel sits on the exact location.

Two days before the fireside was to happen I experienced a dream. Jolene and I were seated upon the rear bench of the old West Bountiful chapel. The relics of the prophet were somewhere nearby. I was waiting in anticipation to address the saints. The chapel was overflowing with people, and the podium seats were occupied. The oak benches were spacious, and one could walk freely without fear of stepping upon someone else. This part fades away.

I look to the left noticing a circular walkway opening into another chapel several times larger than the chapel where I was seated. I look in wonderment as it appears that this chapel is a part of the chapel where I was seated. I could not see a podium. The people are well dressed in pioneer style clothing with many in attendance. I feel overwhelmed. This part fades away.

Again it opens up to my view, and I am seated in the same location yet there is only one chapel. Jolene is next to my side. The pulpit is no longer within my view, and the sword is somewhere nearby. Now I can only view ten rows of benches filled with people on each section before me. Under our bench are two small paper sacks prepared with food and lemonade. The meeting is about ready to start, when suddenly, it fades away.

Again I am in the same location and circumstances. As I look toward my left, a corridor suddenly opens out of a wall directly facing me. Four well dressed men walk in crossing in front of us. Two look very familiar, and I feel that I have seen them before. All are young in appearance and clean shaven. They appear to be watching the people and looking for something. I'm nervous hoping the food under the bench will go unnoticed. They act like they are security guards looking for something that does not belong. They flow between the benches without disturbing the people. They have now inspected eight rows of benches coming closer to our bench. I feel subconscious with the sacks underneath our bench.

Again the four men are walking or flowing across our row heading toward the corridor. One face looks very familiar as he passes by, and the last man stops in front of me. I look into the face of Joseph Bates Noble.

With a large smile he embraces me then whispers in my ear, "God bless you Howard. You are doing a good thing. Keep it up, you will be blessed." He pulls away turns left and then, with a serious face, he follows the other body guards through the corridor wall leaving my presence. The door is shut and I awake.

The thought came to me these four angels are previous body guards to the prophet Joseph Smith and have been assigned to protect the Prophet's Legion sword.

Who Is That Man?

Chapter 33

Samuel Smith

Just who was the body guard with the familiar face? I do know he attended the West Bountiful First Ward fireside. I think you will find the chapter interesting in the way God works.

I've included a statement by Lisa Dayley the author of *The Frozen Trail* and journalist for a weekly newspaper.[1]

"In September 2009 I happened to pick up a book about Joseph Bates Noble (JBN) at Farmer's Corner down the street from my house. I hadn't planned to go into the store but got this terrible chocolate craving – and against doctor's orders – went and bought some. My doctor tells me that if I don't stop eating I'm going to die, die, die of diabetes. All this from a man who has smoked like a chimney stack for the past 65 years.

"I went into the store, made my purchase when I saw the book about JBN. Joseph Smith, the Prophet, gave JBN his Nauvoo Legion Sword shortly before he was killed at Carthage. JBN's family has had it in their possession for 165 years. I had heard of Bates Noble off and on, but it all kind of went in one ear and out the other.

"As I picked up the book, I noticed the author was Howard Carlos Smith. I didn't recognize the name and hesitated to purchase the book. At about that point, I flipped it over and saw to my great delight that this Howard Carlos Smith was in my ward and my friend Jolene's husband! I was thrilled beyond words and had no idea that Howard was a writer. I thought cool! I always try to help out local novelists by doing articles on what they're writing about, and I especially wanted to help someone in my ward.

"I got the appointment on a Saturday. I had been in Pocatello over the weekend and had to rush home to visit with Howard. I had to call him and tell him I was going to be late. I was in a big rush and wasn't feeling especially spiritual. I just wanted to get the story done as I was on deadline. I emphasize I was in a big hurry and just wanted to run in and out.

"I rushed over to Howard and Jolene's and wound up spending a significant amount of time there. While there, Howard told me about all the crazy things that have happened to him while putting this book together. They've had lightening strikes come out of nowhere and people nearly plow into their house as if something or somebody is trying to stop Howard from publishing this book. When the book finally made it to the publisher, the printer had to discard several hundred copies of the book because of a misprint, but they finally got the job done.

"I was shaking my head during all of this and couldn't for the life of me figure out why this was happening. Joseph Smith died more than 160 years ago, and in that time you would think things would have settled down. Why would anybody want to stop somebody from talking about the sword and the prophet? Enough already, was all I could think.

"Shortly before the Prophet Joseph died, there was a price on his head of $1,000 – equal to about $200,000 today – and even after his death there were concerns that the mobers still intended to decapitate his body. And if they could do that with Joseph's own sword it would be even a greater price for the cowards. So the sword was hidden up for decades.

"I had told Howard during our visit that my great-great-grandfather Samuel Smith had also been a body guard to Joseph Smith. I also told him that many people had pooh-poohed that as A LOT of men had served in such a position and what was so special about Samuel? As a result I just brushed off the association, but, of late, I've come across information that indicates that Samuel and Joseph Smith were very close. Joseph Smith greeted Samuel and his family after they arrived in Nauvoo and for some reason they became good friends.

"I finished the interview, took Howard's picture and went on my merry way. Before I left, he asked me if he could review the article. I told him that I don't normally do that as I've done that in the past and everything comes back to me sounding as if an engineer wrote it. It loses my style and sounds like somebody else. Because he's in my ward and to make sure everything was right, I agreed."

The next day I visited with Lisa to review the article and picture for the Weekly Journal. Being an historian for the Smith family, I found it very interesting that her great-great-grandfather was Samuel Smith, not related to Samuel H. Smith brother to the prophet Joseph and Hyrum. You have to be careful not to mix up the two Samuel Smith's in church history.

I was very interested in Lisa's great-great-grandfather Samuel Smith. Shortly following the West Bountiful fireside she provided a history on Samuel Smith by email as well as a picture. As I viewed the picture I about fell off my chair. It was the same body guard that was with Joseph Bates Noble.

Here is a short resume on Samuel Smith a friend to Bishop Noble.

- Baptized December 25, 1841 by Elder Lorenzo Snow.
- He and his family reached Nauvoo January 1843
- Quickly became a friend to the Smith family – Joseph and Hyrum as well as Joseph Bates Noble family.
- Ordained a Seventy and chosen as one of the Presidents. Set apart by Brigham Young's brother Joseph.
- Quickly advanced from a foot soldier to a Second Lieutenant and in 1845 promoted to Captain of the Nauvoo Legion.
- Early 1846 Samuel left with his family from Nauvoo.
- He was among the saints that camped at Mt. Pisgah where two of his children died.
- One time, on the Fox River where they were temporarily stationed, the Smiths were confronted by a mob which had collected to tar and feather Samuel. He met this threat with vigor and determination. He strode to the top of a mound of earth and turned to confront his enemies. "Renounce Mormonism!" they shouted, "and we'll not give ye a black coat and wings."

Samuel did no such thing. Instead, he drew his pistol to defend himself. He then boldly told them that whoever came up that hill to tar and feather him would never live to finish the job. The look of grim determination on his face and the conviction in his voice saved him. After some mutterings and threats the mob retired, leaving him unmolested.[2]

- When they reached Salt Creek, cholera broke out among the people. Many were prostrated by it, and in a few days 18 persons had died of that scourge; others recovered and for a time they thought the plague had left them. When they reached the Platte River, however, the sickness broke out again. "And here," testifies Samuel, "we witnessed some singular instances of healing by the power of God. One night I had a vision. I thought a man stood by me, and said to me: "You must stop here, clean out your wagons, wash yourselves, and all of you be rebaptized and then your sick shall recover and no more death or sickness shall come upon your company." I told my dream to the chaplain and the captain, and they each said they had seen and heard the same thing." After administering to the ailing Chaplain Hunt and then to his own wife, and seeing them instantaneously cured, Samuel continued his account. "After cleaning up, washing and baptisms, this sickness left us; we resumed our journey and reached Salt Lake City in health and safety, on the 5th of September, 1850." (*Tullidge's Histories*, p. 120).
- Later on in the Utah Territory he was called by Brigham Young to help settle Brigham City and the surrounding area.
- Made his home in Brigham City and over the years he had a large family consisting of five wives and fifty-one children.
- A builder of Utah and Mayor for several terms in Brigham City.
- Even to this day he is known in the history books of Brigham City. In the church he was honored and treated as but few men are. His life's labor was crowned by being ordained a Patriarch.

He died on October 2, 1896. I can say with a surety that he is a friend to Joseph Bates Noble.

NOTES:

1. ISBN 978-0-9796070-4-2

2. http://freepages.genealogy.rootsweb.ancestry.com/~rhtuch/famhist/d&ssmith/rhtuch/famhist/d&ssmith/samuel_smith_history_long.html

A Kiss On The Cheek

Chapter 34

My mother taught me the principle of individual prayers starting out as a little boy. I have always followed her council and advice: "Get onto your knees and talk to your Heavenly Father." I don't believe I've missed one day following her example. I believe in prayer it has added many blessings upon my head.

I often think about my grandfather Howard Hellewell. When I was around 10 years of age, he passed away suddenly and unexpectedly. It was a shock to my family. He had just gone in for outpatient surgery in Salt Lake City. A short time later he died, and, as a lad, it greatly upset me.

Shortly after his passing, my grandmother Nancy got sick and came to live with us. I loved my grandma. We were very close – and she spoiled me.Each night I would kneel at my bedside asking my Father-in-Heaven to deliver Grandma from her suffering and sickness. It came to a point where I was having terrible nightmares about her dying. At this age I lacked knowledge of life after death. My grandma being very sick was dying a little bit each day. She had suffered several strokes causing extreme pain with terrible headaches. It really bothered me seeing her so sick.

I remember going to view my grandfather's remains. Grandma took me with her, and the two of us viewed his body by ourselves. It was a special moment for me – a date with my grandma. He looked so peaceful. I remember grandma going up to him with tears in her eyes and kissing him on his cheek.

Later I made a promise to her that I would always stick by my mother in time of need. Looking back at my life, I can honestly say that I kept that promise.

At this time I hesitate to share just a little of a conversation I had with my departed grandpa. Nevertheless, I will share a little for the benefit of those readers who may not believe in a life after death or may lack understanding.

Grandma was under the care of my mother for many months. In those days you didn't place your mother or father in a rest home. Rest homes didn't exist. The doctor made house calls, and, at times, mother would take grandmother up to the medical center for follow-up visits.

One night before bed I knelt in prayer "asking God to bless my dying grandma." Soon under the covers, I went into a deep sleep having one of my normal childhood nightmares when all of a sudden my dream faded away. I was fully awake. Standing at the foot of my bed was my Grandpa Hellewell who had passed away three years prior to this time. I was really happy to see him, and he looked very happy. I felt a secure feeling within my soul being in his presence. He spoke to me, calling me by name and said, "Howard, I have come to spend the night with grandma, and tomorrow, before twelve noon, I will depart taking your grandmother with me. I don't want you to worry anymore because she will be happy where we're going."

Many relatives were visiting at the time of her passing. Early morning I told my parents about my strange experience or visit with grandpa. However they were busy with family and neither one of them seemed to pay much attention.

I went across the street to play with a friend. At five minutes to twelve my sister Sondra ran across the street calling me to come home quickly. I entered the house and found my grandma had just passed away. I knew my grandfather had taken her to a new wonderful world to live where she would suffer no more. Someday, I know we'll meet again just as I now know this is just a testing ground, and my days of mortal probation will end, just like yours. My grandparents' mortal bodies are buried next to each other at the Farmington Cemetery.

A Picture Staring At Me

Chapter 35

During my working years I spent many times getting in and out of airports. At some airport terminals, you must stand tall, and hold tight as a terminal train takes off and stops at a high rate of speed. One time I suddenly realized that I was going the wrong way. Quickly changing directions I made a mad dash with my luggage cart to the next gate, only to find out that I missed my flight or there is a mechanical delay. Another day at the airport, but soon I am on my way.

Shortly thereafter, I'm risking my life standing next to the curb waiting for a Hertz bus. I soon load my luggage on and off again at a high speed to pick up my assigned rental car. Finally, I'm on my way to a motel, park the car, haul my luggage to the lobby, check in, up the stairs to my assigned room only to discover an electronic room card doesn't activate the door. I go back down the stairs, re-program the door card, go back up the stairs, and finally into a new temporary two room house. Oh, I'm so happy, I'm finally home.

Now it's time to check out my new bed. Pulling the covers down I look for possible foreign objects, or good old friends such as bed bugs. It passes inspection. The place is starting to feel like home as I hang up my clothes and place my shaving lotion, etc. onto the narrow sink area. I hop onto the bed and place four flat pillows on top one another to support my stiff neck; I then try to program the television remote buttons only to find out the batteries are dead. So out my door, down the stairs, pick up new batteries, back to my room, install new batteries, jump onto the bed and finally I have many comforts of home - the television turns on. I'm hungry so time to find some food.

Within walking distance from my new house is a family style restaurant. Yes! One with home cooked food. I can hardly wait as I see that the serving area has a large open pit fire place with burning logs. It's an early dinner hour, not many people here and seating is available almost anywhere. A young college waitress seats me at a small table several tables down from the fireplace. Food is on the way.

While waiting on dinner my eyes can't help but notice many old and precious antiques situated on narrow display shelves just above my head. There are many old picture frames of assorted shapes and sizes displaying grandpas, grandmas, husbands, wives and children surviving from a distant time. It reminds me of the many times I have visited antique shops. The pictures seem to be staring at me saying "Why am I here? What happened to my family?" Each one is dressed in their best attire, very formal, fine clothing, one or two sitting upon a horse buggy, a bridesmaid attired for her wedding, a proud dad standing tall, a mother sitting and in her lap a baby boy dressed in a white lacy dress. In the late 1800's a white dress was the attire in picture taking especially for the boys. It was not a statement of one's manhood, just a white dress.

A picture links us to a different time period. It's sad to see that a family member didn't take time to identify the ones in a picture nor to write down dates and location.

It took a lot of effort on the part of that person while posing, a fancy laced dress, a wool suit, sitting on a chair or sofa, or maybe a horse or a dog along side. Some people are holding their favorite family cat. The old picture is someone's family history. The picture represents the strength of our country, a hard working people who stood up for freedom, free agency and put their lives on the line during the great wars.

Deep in thought I glance up to see my student waitress. "I'm back, do you want more water? For dessert would you like carrot cake or ice cream? It comes free with the meal." I say, "How about a piece of pie?" "The peach cobbler just left the oven freshly baked and hot," said the waitress. "Wow that sounds great, could I have it with ice cream on top?" She said she'd be back in a few minutes it was a busy night. I told her no rush I had no place to go just my hotel room – my home away from home.

Pondering once again, I look around staring at pictures. My eyes suddenly center upon a light house. It sits upon a hill next to the ocean. It is a light house within a very old picture frame, probably late 1800's. Sitting there waiting for my peach cobbler, my thoughts soon focus onto my mother. The old light house was a favorite picture of hers. My heart is now heavy; I'm a bit teary eyed. It seems like a day or two ago when mom passed away.

Shortly after this time my daughter Jolene pieced together a puzzle of a light house. It was sitting on a cliff overlooking the Atlantic Ocean. She glued puzzle parts onto a sturdy backboard. It was a special gift to me. The puzzle picture is beautiful, almost looking three- dimensional because it jumps out at you, however at the time it lacked a frame. It is a beacon of light giving direction in life to one lost in the darkness of fog onto a pathway of safety. The puzzle picture was a reminder of my mother. As an amateur painter, one of her favorite paintings was a light house. The puzzle picture now has a frame sporting a spot on our wall.

My daughter Jolene recounts a visit from her grandmother:

September 24, 1993. It was a usual Friday night. We went to a church dance. While there we met a guy by the name of Rulon Waite. Rulon is a return missionary, and also a really nice guy. He later met up with us at the usual Denny's location, for our late night meal. While waiting for our meals, one girl in particular was flirting with Rulon and asked him for his number. So she handed her napkin along with a pen. He wrote down his number, and then began to draw a quick sketch of a dragon. Everyone was in amazement and immediately began handing him their napkins while he sketched quick pictures. I watched carefully and decided to hand to him my napkin also. As I handed it to him I said "Sketch something different for me, other than the dragons and tigers." He said ok! But he kept putting it off. When he finally got to my napkin he took a long time, more than on any other sketch. As I watched diligently, I had no idea what he was sketching. When he finished he handed the picture to me. I stared at it in amazement, for it was the most amazing sketch. It was of a light house on a cliff overlooking the whole entire ocean. We sat and talked for a while and then I took him home thanking him over and over for the wonderful picture. I immediately went home and stuck the picture in my photo album right next to my grandmothers' picture and obituary. The next morning I woke up and began to get ready for my grandmothers funeral. Before leaving my bedroom I glanced one last time at the sketch drawn earlier for me. And then proceeded onward for the funeral. I arrived at the church and began to open the door, when a man greeted me and handed me a program. I thanked him then walked in and signed in at the guest register. As I was signing in I

noticed the programs on the table so I looked at mine. The picture on the program was of a light house on a cliff overlooking the ocean. The same picture that had been sketched for me earlier. I thought it was odd, the program and the sketch were alike. After the services I went home to call Rulon and ask why he drew me that particular picture. He said he didn't know why, it was the only thing that kept coming to mind, he couldn't think of anything else. So I left it at that but often still wonder why. ------Jolene Smith------

As you can see there are two Jolene's in my life - my wife and my daughter. My wife was asked to write an article on Faith for a weekly newspaper. The topic Jolene selected as 'A Mirror Image' with words of faith dedicated to my mother.

I'm sharing just a portion of Jolene's article "A Mirrored Image".

Do things happen by chance or is there divine assistance in many of the instances in our daily lives whether it is for comfort, knowledge, guidance, etc? This question has come to me several times over the years, and I have come to the conclusion that yes, there is divine assistance in our lives many times by the means of God's ministering angels.

I had been an only daughter-in-law for ten years and felt a closeness of sisterhood to my mother-in-law, Verla. It seemed we had known each other a lot longer. We laughed and joked about many things, talked about our lives, the goings-on of our family members and remembrances of times past. We also talked about spiritual things, and we would also joke with each other that whoever passed into the next life first will have to give the other person a sign.

The last five years of her life Verla became ill but never complained. The last few months of her life her closest companion was an oxygen tank. Just before her death my husband, Howard, visited with her quite often. Verla mentioned to him that the Spirit World was very close, and that she had been visited by angels.

After she died, my father-in-law Lee, Howard and I went to the mortuary together to get things finalized. We went through many different styles and pictures for the funeral program. Lee kept on going back to the same picture. When Howard saw it, he made the comment that Verla loved light houses and the ocean.

Lee didn't say anything at that time because I said that we should at least look at everything else so there was no question. Once we looked through all the pictures it was decided that the light house on a cliff overlooking the ocean would be on the front of the program, and the Lord's spirit was felt overwhelmingly.

But there was yet to come a sign to my stepdaughter Jolene that would amaze all of us.

When she arrived at the chapel, she noticed the programs and noticed the picture on the program was of a light house on a cliff overlooking the ocean; the same picture that had been sketched for her earlier. It was a mirrored image of the program.

Coincidence? I don't think so. These experiences and divine assistance were there at a time of need. The experience so affected Jolene that one year later she found a puzzle of the same light house scene, put it together and gave it to us as a picture. When I look at it, I have fond memories of Verla and Lee, who has since passed away, and the amazement in Jolene's voice and eyes of the mirrored image…."

As with my mother, when a righteous family member graduates from this life, it is both an honorable release and a call to new labors. We should remember that on the other side there is a great family reunion with much rejoicing. This farewell and our separation are their reunion and homecoming. I call it a Graduation Day.

I am sure many of you know the veil can be very thin – that angels are people over there who are pulling for us – people who have faith in us, who have great hopes for us, who are hoping and praying that we will measure up.

An Old Rusty Nail

Chapter 36

I remember as a lad digging up an old rusty nail next to our house. My dad, Kenneth, had asked me to dig several fence post holes. A shovel full of dirt two feet under produced a rusty nail. I wondered just how long this unusual nail was sitting undisturbed in the black loamy soil. Our house was constructed in the 1890's – could the rusty nail possibly be that old? To me the nail seemed so useless doing nothing with the passing of time except reacting chemically with its surroundings dissolving into a rusty state of nothingness.

I examined the nail very closely wondering as to its year of origin. The thought occurred to me, do we as people at times in our lives become as a rusty nail, dissolving slowly into a state of nothingness? Our entire life becomes encircled upon self centered physical needs without ever getting to know the spiritual side of our inner self or others.

Yes, a rusty nail is a part of each person nevertheless what really counts is what you do individually with that rusty nail. My youngest son, Michael, taught me a lesson on the value of rusty nails. A little soap and water, a piece of sand paper, and a polishing cloth along with effort on my part will turn the rusty nail into a semi-polished nail. Nailing the nail carefully into a weakened structure adds strength to the whole of the building. The nail has finally found its inner self.

A new nail discarded upon the ground will sit in a state of nothingness waiting its fate with the passing of time. Only within a few hours its surface will become rusty. A shovel full of dirt on top helps to extend its life protecting it from the elements and atmosphere. A nail buried under the earth can stay there many years and rust actually protects its inner self. Soon the inner self of a rusty nail is calling for help waiting for an extended hand.

Some people look upon others who by chance are living on the streets, homeless shelters, mental hospitals, rest homes or assisted living as a rusty nail. They often think about looking you up and making a visit, but they don't for fear of getting rust on them. When in reality, it is they who are the rusty nail. Forgetting ones self and thinking of others, extending a helping hand and working with others in removing the rust of life is one purpose of our creation.

Never pass by a rusty nail. It may need help. Who knows it may be an angel, and you are the rusty nail. It is called charity – thinking of others before self.

Global Warming

Chapter 37

A holiday season soon to be upon us is like Global Warming. It is in the air, it's a part of you, and at times you can feel the warmth within your heart. It is catching just like the flu being passed one to another.

What would the United States be like this holiday season if everyone contacted 'Global Warming'? It's a feeling not just a calendar date. It's a glance between friends, a phrase in a carol, a tree ornament made of popcorn, or a gift you get that you've wanted, a gift you give that you wanted to give, and a sameness around the world in the way people feel.

Over the years, do you remember receiving a card wishing you a "Merry Xmas"? It's time to take the "X" out and put Christ in. Let's not merely whisper "Merry Christmas" with no feeling. Let's shout it out with all our hearts! Let's extend our 'Global Warming' to those around us.

Several years back I lacked 'Global Warming', my heart was cold and like stone. I detested the holidays. To me it was a flowing of money from my empty wallet. My greeting at Thanksgiving was, 'I wish you a Happy Turkey and many more'.

Shortly after the big shopping day, we went out to Chinese dinner at our favorite restaurant. It is a peaceful place and almost always quiet. No tables, just booths with three petitions for privacy. Your posterior always sank in the seat reflecting many years of seating.

The restaurant is overflowing with many people, some are sick with 'Global Warming'. Nevertheless, the spacious room is comparatively peaceful. However, this was soon to change adding to my extreme headache. My left ear is activated with a small hearing aid. The hearing aid allows me to tune into other conversations without them being aware. It all depends upon which way I point my head.

Out of nowhere someone starts whistling holiday songs. My head is now pulsating. It seems like he or she is standing on top our dining table. It's starting to drive me nuts! I can't handle it anymore. It just went on and on and on, never ending. Jolene reminds me to watch my manners and be quiet. It amazed me the number of people affected by 'Global Warming'. All day it's on the television, on the radio and in the local newspapers. You hear about it at the barber shop. It's driving me crazy! The whistling suddenly stops! My plate is empty, and it's time to visit the men's room. Entering the men's room the place is overflowing with others. Out of nowhere I hear the whistling of Christmas songs. The noise is coming out from one of the stall doors. Oh no, what should I do? It's just lingering. I need to quickly escape.

All of the sudden the stall door flings open and out walks a little boy whistling a Christmas song. He was neatly dressed and about the age of six. He walks directly toward me and stops by my feet. He looks into my eyes and says, "Mister, my dad taught me how to whistle. Do you think I am a good whistler?"

I'm speechless. My heart softens and I get tears in my eyes. I could feel 'Global Warming' as I look down upon him. I said, "I'm sure your dad is very proud of you. You're a great whistler."

To this day I still reflect upon the little boy with a big smile. The whistles will always be in my heart.

Time will soon pass, the future will be upon us, and someday a 'Global Warming' of great magnitude, none to be equaled, will circle the earth. It is referred to as the "Second Coming of our Lord Jesus Christ".

Yes, I do believe in Global Warming.

"Prince Of Peace"

By Lynne Millman-Weidinger

Appendix A

The painting "Prince of Peace has been a journey in the making for over five years. It was painted during my most trying times and heartache. So many lessons and experiences had to be learned to be able to capture the emotions of the Savior, who suffered and experienced all things through His atoning sacrifice for all mankind. Because of His love for each of us, He knows our pain and suffering and will carry our burdens if we let Him.

The painting, "Prince of Peace", didn't start until fifteen years after my friend shared a sacred experience with me, where she had witnessed the Savior. She challenged me to paint Him, but I wasn't ready at that time. When the prompting came to start the painting, no model was used, it had to come from inspiration with the help from the Lord as well as help from my friend. She was also going through extreme trials as the painting progressed, and she documented everything that continued to take place during the next five years, and back into our childhood.

Before the painting was completed, there was a feeling of something missing and why would the Lord have me do this painting when things weren't right at home. It was after that, ending up in the hospital for an emergency operation, that I felt the split second of dying. It was a wonderful and indescribable feeling of great relief from everything. It was like a car being lifted off of me, with no worries and no looking back. A few days after that experience, I felt the Lord's hands holding my face and looking into my eyes. The strong feeling of love was all encompassing and tears of joy could not be held back. I knew I was suppose to see the Savior, even though I could not remember what He looked like or what He said. My only guess was that He wanted me to go back to my family to help them, and through faith and inspiration finish the painting. The painting began to change from an earthly Christ to a more Celestial Christ. His face became a more perfected and the color scheme changed throughout the painting.

My greatest trials and lessons were about to begin after leaving the hospital. My trials were so hard and went on for a very long time, keeping me from being able to smile or laugh, or being myself because of the emotional pain and heartache that was felt. It was in the Lord's time, my lessons of patience, long suffering, perseverance, endurance, forgiveness, faith, unconditional love, overcoming fear, not judging others, trusting in the Savior by putting His will first, were learned. I then became a new person having greater strength to overcome adversity and know the Lord is always there. I have a testimony of the power of prayer and that prayers are answered!

What I shared above is a very small part of the journey of this painting. It is an inspirational story about this very special witness of Jesus Christ. The mission of this painting is to heal and bring us back to the Lord and our Father in Heaven and to prepare for the Savior's Second Coming. Our goal is to take this image throughout the world sharing it with all the miracles and trials that have happened and to this day continue to happen.

I testify of Christ, that he lives! He is our Savior and Redeemer. I know that I was commissioned by the Lord to do this painting with His help and the help of my friend. I pray that it will bring comfort to all that see it, to help us in good times as well as in our darkest hours.

www.millmanstudios.com

Wives And Children — Appendix B

A book could be written just about the seven wives of Joseph Bates Noble.

Around 1860, a blessing was given to Joseph Bates Noble by Church Patriarch John Smith.[1] I have included just a small part: *"Joseph Bates Noble, the Lord has had his eyes upon thee through the lineage of thy fathers. For upwards of 400 years thy fathers have had visions of the coming of this work and lived in hopes of seeing it, but have died without the sight."*

"Thou shalt also have numerous posterity on the earth. They shall even excel David and Soloman for strength and wisdom."

"Thy name shall be had in honorable remembrance in the church forever."[2]

<u>The Children of Joseph Bates & Mary Adeline Beman Noble</u>

Meriam Noble
Joseph Heber Noble
Nephi Noble
Louisa Noble
Edward Alvah Noble
Mary Adelia Noble
Hirum Brigham Noble
Eliza Theodsia Noble
Benjamin Noble

<u>The Only Child of Joseph Bates & Sarah B. Alley Noble</u>

George Omer Noble

<u>The Children of Joseph Bates & Mary Ann Washburn Noble</u>

Mary Elizabeth Noble
Tamer Noble
Joseph Bates Noble, Jr.
Hyrum Noble
Alfred Noble

The Child of Joseph Bates & Susan Hammond Ashby Noble

Louisa Adeline Noble

Joseph Bates & Millicent London Noble had no children

The Children of Joseph Bates & Julia Rosetta Thurston Noble

Josephine Noble

Harriet Noble

Sarah Maria Noble

Charles Noble

The Children of Joseph Bates & Sylvia Loretta Mecham Noble

Susan Vilate Noble

Elnora Noble

Bates Mecham Noble

Mary Beatrice Noble

Erastus Alma Noble

Artemesia Noble

Frank Mecham Noble

Loretta Sylvia Noble

William Wallace Noble

Joseph Parley Noble

Zina Pearl Noble

The succeeding generations of Joseph Bates Noble's descendants can be found in a complied volume of family group sheets available at the Genealogical Office in Salt Lake City, Utah; www.new.familysearch.org or other online genealogical sites.

NOTES:

1. Essentials in Church History, by Joseph Fielding Smith, 1950, p 702.
2. A Blessing by John Smith, Patriarch, upon the head of Joseph Bates Noble. Daughters of Utah Pioneers Museum Manuscript Dept.

About the Author

Howard Carlos Smith is a native of West Bountiful Utah and is the author of *Keeper of the Prophet's Sword.* He holds a B.S. Degree in Automotive Engineering from Utah State University and a Master's Degree in Industrial Education from Brigham Young University. He is a research historian in his own family. Many years have been spent as a trainer in industry and secondary educational teacher. Over 15,000 students have attended his classes spanning a period of forty-five years.

He has served in various church positions. One of the highlights of his life was serving a two year mission throughout Florida and Puerto Rico. He was one of three missionaries to open up the island of Puerto Rico for the preaching of the Gospel. He has many stories to share on this topic.

He and his wife, Jolene, share seven children and eleven grandchildren. They reside in Burley Idaho.